A Family Like Mine

A
Family
Like Mine

Biblical Stories of Love,
Loss, and Longing

ROSALIND C. HUGHES

UPPER
ROOM BOOKS®
NASHVILLE

A FAMILY LIKE MINE: BIBLICAL STORIES OF LOVE, LOSS, AND
LONGING
Copyright © 2020 by Rosalind C. Hughes.
All rights reserved.

Upper Room Books® website: upperroombooks.com

At the time of publication all website references in this book were
valid. However, due to the fluid nature of the Internet some addresses
may have changed or the content may no longer be relevant.

Cover design: Jay Smith, Juicebox Designs
Illustration and hand-lettering: Kristi Smith, Juicebox Designs
Typesetting and interior design: PerfecType | Nashville, TN

ISBNs
978-0-8358-1921-3 (print)
978-0-8358-1922-0 (mobi)
978-0-8358-1923-7 (ePub)

Printed in the United States of America

To my mothers

CONTENTS

Contents

INTRODUCTION

Many Mansions

"In my Father's house are many mansions."
—John 14:2, KJV

It was my grandmother's favorite Bible verse. When you read of the vast accommodations of God's mansion, what kind of a household does your imagination build? What kind of people live there, and how do they make out of a household, a home; out of many, a family? How many extensions have been built; or has it always been, like the embrace of God, infinite, standing ready to receive every orphan into a family broader and deeper than creation, as broad and high and deep and enduring as love itself?

At church, the meeting was going well. The enthusiasm and energy were effusive and contagious. The idea of opening up ministries that had been the fiefdom of white-gloved church ladies to families, to children, with their delightfully sticky fingerprints, letting them lay their hands on holy stuff and play church in the actual sanctuary, with the real altar—there was a wild and wonderful Spirit blowing through a normally sedate and staid business meeting. This was what a church should be about! This was what sharing the gospel looked like! I was inspired, flying high, until I was brought down to earth with a bump when someone said, "Families: You know, Mom, Dad, a couple of children . . ."

I do not know when or why society became seduced by the dogma of the nuclear family; its pursuit appears almost as an idolatry. Like other idols, its promise is false; appearances may be deceiving. Despite persistent technicolor expectations of 1950s family tables, uniform in their character call list, we know from our earliest stories that for as long as humanity has understood itself to be, the business of making family has been fraught with duplicity, devotion, murder, and mystery. The human heart is restless until and unless it finds its hearth and home with God, as Saint Augustine once famously Confessed;[1] but long before Augustine, before Paul and Peter, before Moses, even before God called Abram out of Haran, a whole family saga was set in motion with enough false starts, fraudulent friendships, forced family lies and ties to keep a soap opera writing staff in business for millennia—one that was more *The Young and the Restless* than the restless hearts of saints.

Family is complicated, always has been. A family may look to the casual observer like the perfect nuclear nub of shared DNA: Mom, Dad, the children. But in the background, in another room, there is the child effectively orphaned by addiction, by alcohol, by adoption, but fiercely family, never lacking love, if it could be helped at all. "I will not leave you orphaned," Jesus promised (John 14:18). In another room, we find another child of God, the survivor, born by techniques not dreamed of by our biblical ancestors. In ancient days, she would have been thought of as a miracle of divine intervention. She still is.

In the heart of God's household are more orphans, bereaved of their families by abuse and afraid to begin anew, the ones who wear their wounds on their sleeves whenever "family-friendly" activities are announced. "I will not leave you orphaned," Jesus had promised. "I am coming to you. . . . because I live, you also will live" (John 14:18-19).

Sitting stunned by the stark definition that disrupted my spirit in the church meeting that had been going so well, I thought of the family who brought their twin girls for baptism, two mothers beaming with

11

pride and a still-tentative trust that this household of God truly welcomed not only their daughters but also themselves, their marriage, their family. Jesus reassured them, "'Do not let your hearts be troubled. Believe in God, believe also in me. In my Father's house there are many dwelling places. If it were not so, would I have told you that I go to prepare a place for you?'" (John 14:1-2).

Families are complicated, and defining family is a fool's errand. The family defined by law and the one defined by love might overlap, diverge, sing to each other across canyons. My own family background has its own share of drama.

The legal fiction is that I was born to my adoptive parents, who loved me, who gave me at least some of the names I use to this day. It says so on my birth certificate—the one that I submit for passports, driver's licenses, Social Security numbers. I dare say they'll want to see it for my death certificate, when it comes to it. But even my own name makes me nervous, when it comes to official paperwork. I read the stern warnings of perjury and penalty, and I am gripped with an insane guilt: *What if I am accidentally lying, to the paper forms and to myself?*

"Have you ever gone by any other name?" ask the official typefaces. "Have you changed your name by marriage or deed poll?" the block, black ink presses on.

I attach a copy of my birth and marriage certificates to prove my answer. But they do not tell the whole story.

There is another birth certificate, one that was sealed and released into the wilds after I became an adult. It gave me a whole other name, the one I held for a few short weeks, given me by the birth mother who held me briefly and tenderly. Each of us continued to grow up apart, each changing our names, gaining and growing new families to fill in the interrupted story of parent and child, brother, sister, sibling, drawing our families away from the secret of our first days together. We were each of us happy in our own lives; yet I will confess to that restlessness of heart that knows the primal tug of a broken connection, a severed tie, and I could not simply let the secret lie.

Growing up, it was the stories of the Bible that comforted that restless heart, that sustained me with the thread of eternity, the secure assurance that I am exactly who God created me to be, whoever's home I might inhabit, whatever name I may go by. I devoured the stories of Creation, with their poetic declaration: You are from God. "Let us make humankind in our image, according to our likeness," said God in the beginning (or at least, only a few days later) (Gen. 1:26).

I wondered how Hannah, loving Samuel and weeping him into life, could let him go. I wondered what Mary's mother really said when Mary first told her the fears that crept over that missing month, the unanswered call of the moon. I crept into the grave with the psalmist and crawled back out again, blinking at God's glory. I loved the renaming. I loved the way that God claimed the names of those whom God loved: of Sarai, of Jacob.

I loved the story of Hosea's children (see Hos. 1–2). It's a terrible story, really, in which a man marries a woman for whom he has no respect and begets children by her to prove a point and calls them names that further diminish their dignity, their essential virtue—a daughter who is not to be pitied, a son disowned before he has spoken his first word.

Yet God somehow turns even this miserable and banal tale of family dysfunction around. God uses the rejection of the youngest child, *Lo-ammi*, which means "Not my people," to demonstrate God's Spirit of redemption, of constancy, of adoption, calling him instead "My people"—my family, my child. The daughter, pitiful in her pitiless naming, becomes an emblem of God's mercy: *Lo-ruhamah*, "Not pitied," has been restored, rescued, renamed, and reordered by a God who could not for very long leave these infants blowing in the wind, unclaimed and ill-named; who is constitutionally unable to withhold love from God's children or to abandon them. God promises,

Can a woman forget her nursing child,
>   or show no compassion for the child of her
>   womb?
Even these may forget,
>   yet I will not forget you.

(Isa. 49:15)

■　■　■

It was not too long after the creation of humanity, in
the biblical account, that we lost sight of God. Perhaps
Cain, the murderer, was the last to see God face to
face, toe to toe, outside the Garden and heading east
(see Gen. 4). Just as God had questioned Cain's parents
in the Garden, walking in the cool of the evening and
finding them hidden and naked, so God seems to walk
up to Cain, scuffing the ground with one sandaled toe,
stepping dangerously close to the place where Abel's
body and blood cry out from a hastily dug grave. Even
so, God marked Cain as God's own, daring anyone else
to claim revenge against him. For the love of Abel, God
reserved that revenge to Godself. For the love of Cain,
God needed him to get out of God's sight.

By destroying the image of God in his brother, Cain
lost sight of the image of God for himself. By breaking up the family, Cain severed the umbilical cord that

tethered him to God in that first, primal, physically present way.

In its broadest arc, the Bible tells the story of our reunion with the God who is our Creator, Redeemer, and Sustainer, our parent by birth and by adoption, the most complete image of our identity. We are legion, we are many, but God has our seemingly infinite variety covered by God's own infinite image. However we differentiate ourselves, we cannot deny the image of God that imprints us, shaping us in ways our DNA maps cannot describe. Most of the rest of our faith history is the journey back toward that walk with God that our first faith ancestors enjoyed. Through prophets and politicians, kings, judges, and even the odd donkey (see Num. 22), we kept in touch. Moses once even saw the divine backside, disappearing around a corner (see Exod. 33:18-23). In Jesus, we came the closest anyone had since Cain to seeing God face to face. "Whoever has seen me," Jesus told Philip, his disciple, "has seen the Father" (John 14:9).

We are, each of us, made in the image of God, as much God's creatures as the first human, made of the clay of the earth, the *humus* and the breath of God (see Gen. 2:7). At our baptisms, we are told that the voice that spoke to Jesus assures that we too are God's children, well beloved. We are told too that when we cry out, "Abba! Father!" it is the spirit of our adoption crying out within us (see Rom. 8:15-16; Gal. 4:4-6); the cry of recognition of the family of God, stretched between the poles of birth and adoption, creation and redemption, blood and water.

That family history is the gospel that I want to share: the one that tells that we are a reflection of the diversity of the divine creation in which the image of God is refracted in infinite ways not only through our bodies, minds, and spirits but also by our relationships; that in the household of God there are many rooms, and there is room for every last child made in the image of God's love.

The intricate and interlacing patterns of family; the mirrored themes of love, loss, and longing; these run throughout the stories of our spiritual ancestors—nothing is left out. Within the grand acts and arias of the Bible, the whole of human experience is laid bare, and within its cadences, its syncopated rhythms, its lyric moments, its polyphonic harmony and discord, we find our own family history, suspended somewhere between grief and glory.

Questions for Reflection

- When you read of the many mansions, or dwelling places, in the household of God, what image does that conjure in your faithful imagination?
- Whom do you see living there? Who is missing?
- Where is God?

HOW TO USE THIS RESOURCE

This book has been a lifetime in the making. The first inklings I had of Something, Someone called God were nurtured and watered by the stories of the Bible and by the imaginative qualities of prayer, that conversation that stretches beyond all known borders.

The stories of the Bible are our family stories. Inspired and true, essential and authentic, they are the memories of our spiritual ancestors. Memories are living creatures. Each time we read a memory in the Bible, it takes on a new life within us.

The retelling of biblical stories contained in this book owes much to the inspiration of poetry. I have played with and prayed with details implied by or even imagined to be hiding behind the plain text of the characters explored in this book. Perhaps that is one way of continuing the work of those family story-gatherers who gave us the sacred texts that still today tell us the truth about God's love for this world that God has made and for us, made in the spitting image of our Creator.

My own earliest memory consists of a lot of emotion and surprisingly little narrative. It turns out that this is because it is from a time in my life when I had yet to learn to string words together in any reliable fashion. Its story remains, to the best of my memory, true. I have tried to tell true stories in this book.

The people of the scriptures made room for variations on a theme; for trial and error; for the mysteries of love, loss, and longing. I have found deep comfort, fellow-feeling, and faithful companionship through the complicated histories of my spiritual ancestors and the simplicity of their overarching message: God loves you.

I encourage you, whether in a group or alone, whether through the reflection / discussion prompts at the end of each chapter or freeform, to let your prayerful imagination feed and be fed by the stories of our shared family, the children of God. Let their stories read you and remind you of the hope and mercy that God has for you, even in the valley of shadows and on the mountaintop. Take your share in their sorrows, struggles, and joy, and let them lead you always back to the kernel of love that was complete from before the beginning of Creation. Whoever you were made to be, however you became the person reading this book, God delights in every detail of you and loves you without end.

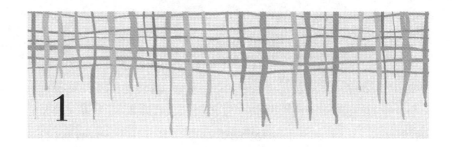

All in the Family: Abraham, Isaac, and Lot

As usual, it was a child who called out the scant nakedness of the story set before us. At the end of the school year, one Sunday school teacher had the idea to assemble the questions the children had asked over the year that, for one reason or another, their teachers had deferred or declined to answer, and to pose the questions to me, their priest, instead. To be fair, it was mooted as a private event in the classroom. I was the one who suggested we do it out in the open, at sermon time, on the sanctuary steps.

Some of the questions were emailed in advance—fortunately, because it gave me a chance to do some research on, for example, how many rectors I had followed into my current position, and how, why, and when the devil was created.

After we had dispatched the simpler stuff, I asked what other leftover questions the children had. One wise soul piped up, "If we all came from Adam and Eve, and we are all one big family, how does that even work? Because I know you can't marry your own sister!"

Fortunately, I have had some practice at turning childish honesty into family-friendly fare. We agreed that, while the Bible tells us the truth about God's creation, love, and faithfulness toward us, it doesn't necessarily tell the whole story of everyone and everything that has happened under God's creative watch. There wouldn't be enough pages in the world to hold such a record! The stories of Adam and Eve and their family, we concluded, describe how we are all descended from the image of God and how we are related, are in relationship, with one another; they don't have to spell out exactly how.

There were different levels of satisfaction with that conclusion around the room, but no one pressed the point further. Some of the grown-ups might have been remembering that our family history includes some very dubious episodes, which we might not want this young person to call into question in front of the altar any time soon.

Long after Adam's family, but long before so much more, God called Abram out of Haran, and a family saga was set in motion, littered with love, betrayal, identity crises, intrigue, incest, and subject to a whole lot of interpretation.

It is no small thing to become the ancestor of three major religions and countless tribes, languages, and nations. But Abram himself was rootless and restless, born in Ur of Chaldea, uprooted by his father to follow the River Euphrates far north, settling in Haran, where he and his wife bedded down into their middle age with no drama to report, no controversy to chronicle until decades had passed and their father had died and their nephew, Lot, was himself fully grown (see Gen. 11:31-32).

Whenever I read about Abraham in that later letter to the Romans with its wicked aside, "He did not weaken in his faith when he considered his own body, which was already as good as dead (for he was about a hundred years old)" (Rom. 4:19), I remember a conversation I once had with a young child of the family. "How old is Great-Grandma?" she asked. "Ninety-something," I replied. "Oh," innocence announced, "she's nearly dead, then."

Abram was neither young nor flighty when the call came through, but he was sprightly. Seventy-five years old, Abram and Sarai had long since celebrated their golden wedding anniversary in Haran when God called them out of retirement and a peaceful sunset and set them adrift on the shifting sands of the Negev desert.

Abram had heard that he was to become the father of nations, but he had not heard of, nor had he read, the letters that they would write about him later, asserting that even though he was as good as dead, his faith was of such vibrant strength and certainty that it was reckoned to him as righteousness. They wrote as though he never wavered or quavered in his trust in the promises and providence of God.

But back in the day, Abram was hedging his bets. He appointed a servant of his household as his heir and took his nephew along for backup. Scripture declines to describe how Lot felt about his uncle's preferment of a hired hand over himself as heir; but he and his uncle would part ways after Egypt (see Gen. 13).

Abram did not deal well with tension. His form of faith was more about "letting go and letting God" than facing the stars with a promise of persistence. He was a master of giving up and giving away, of leaving. When his relationship with his brother's son reached a fork in the road, he took it. His own firstborn, at a word from his wife, he sent into the wilderness with nothing but a mother and a loaf of bread and water (see Gen. 21:9-14). He made a show of sadness, it is true; but he did not fight for Ishmael, nor for the child's mother, Hagar. And have you heard of his other wife, Keturah, and her six sons? He gave them gifts and sent them away (see

Gen. 25:1-6). When others desired Sarai, he willingly gave her to them, telling her to keep his secret, to go along with his betrayal, his sacrifice of her faithfulness to his vision of his own journey of faith.

Picture the scene in Genesis 12:10-20, in an encampment on the edge of the Negev, many hundreds of miles from home. I imagine that Sarai was making the best of a bad situation. Her husband, she surmised, must have gone mad, to think that their time of life was suitable for a fresh start.

Sarai had been a good wife, even if she had been unable to turn his urges into an heir born of her own flesh and blood. But you cannot be married for sixty years or so without a few wrinkles emerging along the way. For a long time now, Abram had ceased to treat her as a woman, as a wife; she could have been his sister or his servant or a stranger. So, when he suggested that she pose as his sister before the court of Egypt, to save his old skin, she would have seen right through him. *Two can play that game,* she might have thought, and washed her face, and painted its shadows with youth, and hung gold from her ears and neck, and covered her gray hair and her gently folding body in desirable cloth. As satisfied as Abram was with her bride price or dowry, she herself settled by stealth into the women's chambers, happy to exchange the desert sand for a life of luxury.

No, it was not necessarily the dedication of Abram and Sarai—renamed Abraham and Sarah by God—to their cause that brought God's promise to fruition, God's family to birth.

We are used to Abraham's example as a man whose great faith "was reckoned to him as righteousness" (Rom. 4:22, after Gen. 15:6). And Abraham had the faith in God to leave behind his home, his family, his nephew, his son, his other sons, his wife. Faith has often been the excuse for his most inexplicable, inexcusable behavior: faith; obedience; dedication.

It sometimes seems as though God made all of Abraham's excuses for him: saved Sarah from the pharaoh and Abimelech (see Gen. 12:10-20; 20:1-18), Hagar from the desert (see Gen. 21:15-19), Ishmael from abandonment (see Gen. 21:20), Isaac from the knife and the fire (see Gen. 22:1-14).

It is commonplace to observe that Isaac's mother, Sarah, does not speak in the Bible again after her husband descends from Mount Moriah with her only son, unsinged but surely scarred by his experience upon the altar, when Abraham had him carry the wood for his own funeral pyre up the mountain and held a knife up between his eyes and the midday sun, as though to kill him. Despite all that she knew already of Abraham's ability to use his family to shield his own skin, or perhaps because of it, Sarah has it left within her only to die (see Gen. 23:1-2).[1]

In the Islamic tradition, it is Ishmael who is the subject of his father's faithful attempt on his life. In Judaism, followed by Christianity, it is Isaac. In a small chapel at a children's school in Al-Salt, in the Hashemite Kingdom of Jordan, hangs an icon that rewrites the story once more, combining traditions, compounding the terror and its resolution. In the icon, rendered in bright hues, Abraham looks younger than his hundred-odd years. He holds his young son, Isaac, by the hand, while his other hand rests on the shoulder of the youth, Ishmael. Behind them rests the bundle of sticks to light a fire beneath the stone altar. "But where is the lamb for a burnt offering?" asks a child, once more laying bare the situation (Gen. 22:7). Further back still, we find the ram of God, caught in a thicket. Above them all, an angel. Although Abraham inclines his head toward his elder son, none of the three looks at another.

A couple of hundred kilometers south of the school and its icon, in the plains to the east of the Dead Sea, Abraham's nephew Lot now lived with his wife and daughters in the city of Sodom, which was a rough neighborhood, by biblical account. When two strangers came through the city gates late in the day with plans to camp out in the city square overnight, Lot knew that this was a recipe for disaster, and having been well disciplined in the habit of hospitality, he insisted that they come home with him (see Gen. 19).

When the townspeople came to abuse the strangers, to teach them not to trespass on their turf, Lot defended them. But he went further than barricading the door. He offered up his own daughters as a sexual sacrifice to appease the crowd.

What their mother said is not recorded, but something in her was broken that night. When the family left town the following day, salvaged by the angels and the bartered mercy of God, I imagine that she was weeping so hard, her very essence evaporated. By the time she turned to take one last look at the scene of her husband's most hospitable crime, all that was left of her was salt (see Gen. 19:26).

Their daughters survived, now orphaned by their mother's petrification and Lot's unfatherliness. Believing their entire world to have been destroyed, they even used Lot's alienation from them as a cover for the kind of family embrace that would make the problems of Adam and Eve and their generations pale into the mists of prehistoric myth (see Gen. 19:30-38).

"Do not presume to say to yourselves, 'We have Abraham as our ancestor'" [warns John the Baptizer]; "for I tell you, God is able from these stones to raise up children to Abraham" (Matt. 3:9).

To claim that we are children of Abraham (let alone Adam and Eve) is to recognize that there are hidden dangers in turning over the leaves of the family Bible and laying bare our spiritual family tree. I always advise parishioners excited about new, commercial DNA testing that advertises closer family bonds and new cousins to be wary, lest they uncover secrets about themselves and how they came to be that they would rather not know. Our physical, our metaphysical, and our faith formation may be complicated by our family history.

Trying to get inside other people's families is a fool's errand. But as my Sunday school student might point out, Abraham's family is our own. His battle with faith over cynicism is our own war with disappointment. The tears of Lot's wife sting our cheeks with their salt. The despondency of Hagar is our fear. The terror of Isaac cries out from the heart of every child of God at one time or another. And our faith is challenged to believe that God will provide a ram to save us from the fire.

But ours too is the occasional laughter of Sarah, surprised by the advent of Isaac, called "the laughing one," for the folly of his parents' old age (Gen. 21:1-7); for laughter is often the only appropriate response to the unexpected, unanticipated, uninvited grace of God that makes its home among us.

The Bible leads us through the stories of our spiritual ancestors—Abraham and the others—into relationship with the One who knew us before Creation began. There is room in the stories for mystery. There is room to maneuver between nature and nurture; the Word of God is a great creator of space, a fine choreographer of connections. The example of Abraham—messy, frequently in error, yet with a faith that was reckoned to him as righteousness—has been reckoned to me as encouragement in a family system that is beautifully complicated by birth and adoption, its patterns reworked and interwoven across generations and genealogies.

Faith is confidence that there is One who knows all of the complications and conflicts of our lives, the naked truth of our origins, our families, and our future, who has resolved them by God's steadfast loving-kindness toward all of God's children; it is that faith that allows me to write this book and that allows me to look a child in the face before the altar and tell him that no matter how confusing it gets, the message of the gospel is always that God loves her, that she is made for goodness, that they are part of God's mysterious and complicated family.

Even if we had never found our way into this life, into these names, into the church, into the families that raised us, then the God who can raise up children from rocks would have known us, and found us, and named us. For that, we give thanks and praise.

For if we were silent, God would raise up children's voices from the stones to cry out instead (see Luke 19:40).

Questions for Reflection

- What does the concept of "biblical family" mean to you? What baggage does it carry, and what blessings?
- Where is your family of origin, of accident, or of choice reflected in the family stories of the Bible?

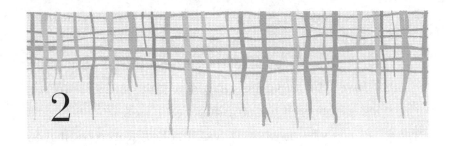

2

A Cautionary Tale

Finding family in the Bible is not for the faint-hearted, although it does come with its own rewards: the cloud of witnesses that supports and encourages our faith.

I didn't grow up in a religious household. There was no theological instruction, no talk of prayer nor visible practice of it. There was a careful, superstitious avoidance of outright blasphemy; euphemistic cursing was the rule of the day. Pretty much the only time God was mentioned was in a classical song. Jesus was confined to his crib, the baby in the manger, meek and mild.

I didn't grow up in a religious household, but I did grow up in a country where church was part of the establishment. Day by day, at public school, I heard stories of Samuel, the prophet, and Saul, the Lord's first appointed and anointed king; of David and Goliath; of Noah, Joseph, and Joshua. There were surprisingly few strong female leads. Jesus, for the most part, remained in his cradle.

When I was about six, Mr. Jones, the headmaster, whom I loved because he gave out gold stars from his office, led a series of assemblies dedicated to the Lord's Prayer. Phrase by phrase, it was broken down to fit into the mouths of babes and sucklings, such as we were. I do not remember his explanation of the word *hallowed*, but I remember the feeling, awestruck and expansive, that opened my soul to the first inklings of a God with a name.

I do not remember what Mr. Jones said to translate the arcane words of an Aramaic street preacher, by way of Thomas Cranmer and King James, to a bunch of English six-year-olds sitting cross-legged on the lunchroom floor; but I remember my heart melting, falling open, beginning to fall in love with such a God who came with a name of God's own: *Abba*.

After my family and I moved away and everything changed, those public-school assemblies were about the only thing that stayed the same.

I have often heard it said that adoption is built upon loss. When I began my search for that spirit of adoption that causes a child of God to cry, "Abba! Father!" (Rom. 8:15; Gal. 4:4-6), the journey that I took to church was built on a young child's growing realization that life involves death, trust can be broken, and some changes are irrevocable.

It started a year before my family moved. I had been outside playing; we lived in a village full of green space and trust. I came home to find my family in tears around the telephone. "Grandpa died," someone told me. I wasn't entirely sure what that involved at the time, what depths those words plumbed; but everyone was crying, so I did too.

By the summer, we had moved away from the village and the hilly fields and the safe spaces in between. We moved away across the toll bridge that made me carsick, to an unfamiliar house with roses in the front yard and elderly neighbors on every side. As penance for moving us, I made my parents get a dog.

It was an unhappy time. My father was irritable; his new job was not a comfortable fit. My new schoolmates were unwelcoming, and I did not curry any favor with them. My mother, buckling under the weight of the unhappiness that she carried for us all, suffered what was still being called a nervous breakdown.

After we moved, the stories, the songs at school, the quiet moments of prayer—"hands together, close your eyes"—these were the threads to which I clung for dear life itself, when life had turned upside down, swinging as it were from the heavens.

One of the stumbling blocks for a child seeking the inheritance of God's adoption is the innate and imprinted knowledge that such ties, in this life, are breakable.

Even God, according to the Bible, has been known to regret taking someone in, taking someone on, as happened to Saul when he fell afoul of a jealous God. Like a sorry, sobbing child pleading with his mother not to leave him, Saul clings to Samuel's robe, a grown man dragged along the ground like a tormented toddler, until the very fabric is torn, and the rent is irreparable (see 1 Sam. 15:26-27). Samuel is sad. God is sorry. Saul ends up going mad.

Even so, a year after we moved, I risked taking myself to the back pew of a church on the wrong side of the toll bridge, and I waited for God to find me there.

■　■　■

In the Acts of the Apostles, Jesus-follower Philip is swept up by the Spirit, who engineers an encounter with an Ethiopian eunuch interested in scripture (see Acts 8:26-39). I am encouraged to envision the man reading from the scroll of the prophet Isaiah when Philip hits the ground running alongside his racing chariot. Philip's divine transportation may account for his ability to keep pace with the horses while asking, casually between breaths, "Whatcha reading?" Just as improbable as

Philip's arrival on the scene is the man's eager embrace, inviting this strange hitchhiker into his car to explain to him the meaning of the scroll in his hands.

Impulsive-yet-wise eunuch! The Bible can be a minefield for the unsuspecting tourist. The accidental injuries caused by friendly fire—a word left in the trigger position with the safety off—can require a lifetime of rehab.

Imagine reading alone for the first time the authoritative opinion of the Deuteronomist that a man with damaged genitals—a eunuch like this one—may never enter the congregation (Deut. 23:1). As a child, I felt a strong kinship with him when I read in the very next verse that a person born out of an illegitimate union— outside of the law, outside of wedlock, outside of the approval of society—is to sit on the bench outside, next to him. The King James Version is uncompromising: "A bastard shall not enter into the congregation of the LORD; even to his tenth generation shall he not enter into the congregation of the LORD" (Deut. 23:2, KJV). That is not a welcoming message to a child of uncertain, uncivil, or unsolicited birth. And there have been so many kinds of uncertain and uncivil birth defined throughout the generations.

But such laws are subject to change, within and without the Bible.

Remember Lot's daughters. Their children's children, the Moabites and the Ammonites, were once, like the eunuch, and me and mine, to be excluded by law from the assembly of the Lord, even to the tenth generation; moreover, "You shall never promote their welfare or their prosperity as long as you live" (Deut. 23:6). But Saul was succeeded as the Lord's anointed by David, whose great-grandmother was a Moabite, Ruth, a daughter of Lot's daughters (see Ruth 1:1-5; 4:17-22); and Ruth's great-great-grandson Solomon built a Temple for the ark of the Lord and entered it (see 1 Kings 5–8).

The legislation covering my own birth records after adoption was revised while I was still a child. A process that had once been considered secret and sealed for all time was opened up so that it became possible for an adopted child to request his or her original birth certificate after attaining adult status. The arrangement was not reciprocal: Birth parents were not permitted to seek out their offspring. If there was to be any kind of reconciliation with my own birth mother, I would have to be the one to begin it.

Before I was allowed to read my own original birth details, I was invited to attend a mandatory interview with an official government social worker. I traveled by train across the country to a bleak prefab building with institutional dirt in the corners of the windows and carpets of the kind that start out threadbare so that there is nothing to ruin. The woman herself was spare and lean, with just enough of her present in body and soul and wire glasses to get the job done. It is not comforting to realize that, what with the cutbacks in recent years, she may no longer have a job at all.

She was not here, she said, to give or to withhold permission to see my birth certificate, which was my right under the present law, still less to offer free advice or counseling. She was not concerned with the accidents of fate that might arise from rejection or the discovery of a parent dead, in prison, or surprised into a sudden stroke by the arrival of a long-lost child. Her only task was to warn me, as a service to public health, about the dangers of genetic sexual attraction. There is, she explained, a condition in humanity that likes to see itself reflected in the other, that warms to recognition, a sight of home behind the lens of another eye. When family history has not established sufficient taboo, a brother, a sister, an aunt or such may find herself unduly drawn to an inappropriate object of sexual affection, and so give birth to an abomination.

I promised her faithfully that I would not fall in love with a relative stranger. She sniffed, as though she could hardly be expected to believe me, statistics being what they are; but she handed over the papers for which I had traveled so far: a birth certificate in another child's name, with a mother but, almost biblically, no father.

As to my biblical brother-in-law, the Ethiopian eunuch, this esteemed official of the court of the queen is in his chariot coming down from Jerusalem. He has been up to the Holy City and its Temple to worship; despite ancient prohibition, he hungers for the living God. The exclusions of a particular time and place do not always apply; and while many of our own religious rules and rituals come and go, it is well known that the grace of God is eternal. The man thinks he will risk it.

But, "What are you reading?" Philip asks the Ethiopian official. It is this:

"Like a sheep he was led to the slaughter,
   and like a lamb silent before its shearer,
      so he does not open his mouth.
In his humiliation justice was denied him.
   Who can describe his generation?
      For his life is taken away from the earth."
                    (Acts 8:32-33, after Isa. 53:7-8)

Were these verses thrown at him as a slur by someone? Or did he happen across them by accident? Either way, Philip looks at this man before him, a eunuch, a shorn lamb. He hears the silent bleating, the weeping of one for whom generation is out of the question, whose life will end with him, and whose name will be buried with his ancestors.

Gentle companion on the journey, starting with the ancient scrolls, Philip explains to the eunuch that the first law was not to describe who was in and who was out of the family. It was not even "go forth and multiply." It began with the first word of God: "Let there be light" (Gen. 1:3).

Carefully, generously, Philip enters into the open wound of this man's life and salves it, smearing it with the gospel, assuring him that God has never been inclined to leave anyone out in the night alone. Like the shepherd who leaves the ninety-nine branded sheep safely in the pen and sets off after the stray, God gathers in the lost and the lonely, the disconnected, the deserted, the desperate (see Luke 15:3-6).

So, in my imagination, Philip tells the eunuch, who leaps full-footed into the promises Philip offers, demanding baptism into his family without further delay. Out of the great cloud of witnesses to God's mercy, God sends traveling companions, unlikely hitch-hikers on our journey through scripture, to help us find our home in the sometimes unfamiliar, even scary wilderness of the Bible and our family history.

After I found my way to church, a man called Mr. Evans appointed himself my godfather and watched over me for the next ten years, until I left for college. He taught me to read the Bible from the lectern, in the midst of the congregation. He encouraged me to become an acolyte, kneeling next to the boys. He said the Grace over the meal at my wedding. He made sure there was a home for me in the household of God.

■　■　■

Around the time of my cross-country journey to that bleak, Eastern Bloc building with its bare walls and spare social worker, a tree that was a graft gone wrong grew in my family's back garden. Sometimes, in order to breed new trees, the root stock of one is used to support the new growth of another. The grafted tree uses the root system of its host to establish itself and grow, and you would not normally know any difference between it and a tree that had grown from its own, original root. But in this tree, the graft had not been properly tended, and the host tree had grown up with the graft, so that the lower half of its canopy was pure white blossom, and above a clear dividing line it was dark pink. It was, to the eye used to the rule of one tree at a time, a strange-looking hybrid.

But really, it was simply a tree that was more honest than its neighbors about its complicated history—a little more expressive of the complexity of the genetic deals, adoptions, and compromises that underlay its identity than most. It was an abominable tree, blooming without shame.

Questions for Reflection

- Which parts of the Bible are hard for you to read?
- Who helps you to face difficult episodes in our shared family history?
- How might the gospel of the whole Bible help to redeem your own story?

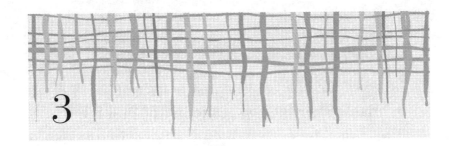

3

Complications:
Rachel Unconsoled

It seems strange that the townspeople of the Bible should see another's childlessness as a sign of divine disfavor, when evidence to the contrary is scattered throughout the stories. Sarah, the promised vehicle for Abraham's sandstorm of descendants, was barren well beyond the remarking of any of her gossipy peers. Hannah was the favorite of her husband, despite her empty womb and open arms. Zechariah and Elizabeth were explicitly blameless, before the angel challenged Zechariah's credulity and rendered him speechless with the annunciation of a long-unexpected baby. Why should the people gossip about any man's dedication to his duty or about any woman's appeal to her God or to her husband, when it is evident that childbearing is not, in fact, her salvation from all sorrow?

> He gives the barren woman a home,
>   making her the joyous mother of children.
> Praise the LORD!
>
> (Ps. 113:9)

It is a bold claim, with a bitter flipside—one that Jesus is not shy of flipping:

> Jesus turned to them and said, "Daughters of Jerusalem, do not weep for me, but weep for yourselves and for your children. For the days are surely coming when they will say, 'Blessed are the barren, and the wombs that never bore, and the breasts that never nursed.'"
>
> (Luke 23:28-29)

■ ■ ■

My own mother was known, for the most part, as a joyful woman. With her ready smile and easy song, she was often the life of the party. It was not until I was old enough to have children of my own that she began to confess her regret, her abiding grief at never having

harbored a child in her own womb, never having suck-
led an infant at her abundant bosom.

It was a cruel irony. She went to school to become
a nursery nurse, a specialist in the care, feeding, and
nurture of small children. Everyone who knew her
knew of her love for children. She was "Auntie Ann"
to half of the neighborhood. She was overflowing with
nursery rhymes and potty-training wisdom, games and
education. She used to bake once a week and let us lick
the wooden spoon clean of sugar, chocolate, butter fat.
Her kitchen was a popular destination.

Like Zechariah and Elizabeth before them, but with
less incense and fewer angels, my parents had led a
blameless life. There was scandalous precedent in the
family that they were anxious not to repeat. After a white
wedding, for the first three years of their marriage, they
lived in rented rooms on an old estate and practiced
careful, cautious sex, even now avoiding an indecently
hasty pregnancy. They saved for a deposit on one of the
new houses being built near the little lake; they bought
the one at the bottom of the hill, closest to the duck pond.
At night, their cat would go fishing, so that on at least
one occasion, they woke up to something slimy and wet,
flapping and flopping across the bedclothes.

Caution thrown to the wind, they invited and
expected new life to visit their new home. But months

turned to seasons, and seasons to years, and still the only gifts of life brought into the house were the dubious offerings of the cat. They consulted doctors. The doctors put my mother on the Pill, hoping that a surge of fertility would follow an enforced barren season. My mother conceived a deep vein thrombosis but no child.

She became bitter, she told me, over the wasted years of safe, scared-straight sex; jealous of friends whose bellies and breasts swelled, whose babies were taken out in their prams for walks around the duck pond at the bottom of the hill.

There is no fairness, it seems, in family planning. Whether tricked by fate or a greedy father-in-law (Jacob had only meant to marry one daughter and work seven years for her dowry, but Laban had other plans [see Gen. 29:15-30]), there is an irony in the delicate balance of fertility that blesses one woman with an unexpected gift for procreation, while another suffers silently as the curse continues month by month without remission.

Leah suffered the humiliation of a succession of children who failed to become their father's favorite. Jacob did not even involve himself with their naming. Leah, knowing herself to be the second-best first wife, poured her heart and hope into their flesh and fingers, counting each one through sweat and mucus. Reuben, named for his father's attention: "See, I have borne you a son!" Simeon, a rebuke to the gossips: "I hear you; and

God has heard how you treat me and mine." Levi, the hat trick scored, born in a paling push for hope: "Now, surely, my husband will love me." Spitting bitterness like spawn, however many more children she bore, Leah was not rescued from her own sorrow, nor from her sister's rivalry, by childbirth (see Gen. 29:31–30:21).

There is an element almost of comedy in the back and forth of Leah's and Rachel's competitive breeding, but it is a cruel kind of comedy. The children's names map out the moods of their mothers' struggle, their despair, their wanton desire for love. Rachel resorts to the prostitution of her maid, receives a son, and judges herself redeemed; yet her own womb remains empty and untried. There is a hunger that is unassuaged, and one child does not undo the grief of so many moons under which she wept. Even when the drought is broken and her waters break over Joseph, she names him for that hunger, saying, "May the LORD add to me another son!" (Gen. 30:24).

In a final act of irony, God does. "Give me children, or I shall die!" Rachel had said once to her husband, and she dies giving birth to Ben-oni, "Son of my sorrow," although his father, finally pricked into paying attention to the game, renamed him Benjamin, to save him from carrying his mother's grief as his own throughout his days (see Gen. 35:16-18).

When my mother did finally fall pregnant, it was ectopic. Instead of traveling to her womb, the fertilized egg attached to the wall of her Fallopian tube, and the emergency surgery that saved her life also took the pregnancy and half of her fertility. The hope of any future pregnancy, let alone its success, was severely reduced. My parents were advised to begin to explore other options.

(One wonders how Bilhah and Zilpah, Leah's and Rachel's handmaids, heard those pregnant words, "other options," hiding behind the modesty screen, handling the fertility issues of the chosen family, exchanging knowing glances, their smocked dresses stained with the milk and vomit of infants who were their own and not their own. Unburdened by the promises of greatness bestowed upon Hagar and her offspring, they were barely heard from again.)

Just before they moved away from the duck pond and the house at the foot of the hill, my parents began their family planning anew, with borrowed hope for a baby—my future brother—soon to be adopted as their own.

■ ■ ■

For no good reason, I was convinced that I would take after my biological parents when it came to fertility. I also deeply desired a child. I found the waiting at times almost unbearable, as though I were grieving a child that should be filling my belly and my heart with its life, even before there was any chance (beyond miracle) that one could have come into existence. Infected, perhaps, by my adoptive mother's empty womb and the unseen memory that severed me from my umbilical mother, I think too that I thought I could redeem both their stories—my mothers and their inconvenient wombs—if I could get it "right" myself; that, as Paul once wrote to Timothy (both men, I now notice), "She"—or in my case, *they*—"will be saved through childbearing" (1 Tim. 2:15).

At any rate, I was by no means surprised to find, on our first wedding anniversary, that small blue line on the home pregnancy test stick: positive. But a couple of months later, my celebration turned sour.

My doctor was not too concerned at first. Objectively, she reasoned, at the three-month mark, hormonal changes often provoke subjectively worrying symptoms. "Take it easy over the weekend," she recommended. "Call me Monday."

By Monday, she was a little more concerned. "Go get an ultrasound," she told me. "I'll let them know you're on your way."

At the hospital, in that darkened cubicle lit by a glowing computer monitor, I saw my little love for the first and only time. Its image was perfect: a bright sea horse in a dark salt sea; a textbook picture on the screen, holding perfectly still, all too tightly defined.

The technician told us that the end had occurred maybe three weeks earlier. Three weeks in which

October had cooled to a November chill. Thirty rush-hour train journeys into the workaday city and home again, jiggety-jig. Three weeks of ginger snap biscuits in my desk drawer, nibbling away the nausea that—who knew?—was no longer needed. Three weeks to give my husband a chance to imagine becoming a father, to begin to plan for a nursery. Medically, it was what they called at that time a "missed abortion." The procedure that followed went in my chart as the "removal of the remaining products of conception," which hardly seemed to cover the loss. After the surgery, in the recovery room, a young woman was crying, screaming. "Is it gone?" she wailed, over and over. "Is it gone?"

For our part, we called it a death, although there were no remains, no memorial.

My mother once told me that she missed the days of knowing, the days of hope, when her second ectopic pregnancy announced itself only at its ending. I could not comprehend her brave optimism. Three weeks of false expectation left me bitter at my body's betrayal. I felt tricked into loving something that was no longer possible, someone who had already left me, without so much as a touch to say good-bye. My first experience of pregnancy shook my confidence both in my biological predestination and my ability to rescue and redeem our collective narrative of birth, of family.

It was the beginning of winter. In our backyard the bonfire of a freshly felled tree stood in place of a funeral pyre. I watched its embers threaten the night sky with their dull glow, then fall back to earth extinguished.

Paul wrote to Timothy that the woman "will be saved through childbearing," but I was in no position to save myself, let alone anyone else. The doctor who signed my certificate for a few days off work asked me about blame. Did I blame myself? Did I blame God for my miscarriage?

■ ■ ■

A tragic and terrifying trial by ordeal is set out in Numbers 5 for a woman suspected by her husband of infidelity. A man seized by "a spirit of jealousy" (Num. 5:14), whether justified or not, may bring his wife to the priest for testing. The priest makes a ritual offering of grain brought by the husband and administers to the woman a potion of dust, water, and written curses washed into the water (see Num. 5:16-26). If she is innocent, all will be well with her and her womb. If guilty, the curses contained in the mixture will cause her womb to discharge and her uterus to drop (see Num. 5:27-28). In other words, it seems, if she is pregnant by adultery, the ritual is designed to diagnose her deceit and cause a miscarriage.[1]

I feel as though I can almost see the woman standing before the priest with her fear and her husband's grain offering in her hands. The priest sets her before the LORD like a chess piece on a board. He dishevels her hair, invading her most personal space without permission or pity. He arranges her hands at the ends of her arms, bends the elbows, straightens the wrists. He places in her hands her husband's grain offering of jealousy. She is still, petrified.

The priest believes that she is as likely to be condemned as to be saved by her childbearing. He makes the woman take an oath, saying:

> "The LORD make you an execration and an oath among your people, when the LORD makes your uterus drop, your womb discharge; now may this water that brings the curse enter your bowels and make your womb discharge, your uterus drop!" And the woman shall say, "Amen. Amen."
>
> (Num. 5:21-22)

I feel indignant for the woman before the priest. I want to jump in and dash the cup from her hand, this woman, so passive, impassive, with her swelling womb and her outrageous husband, her pitiless priest. The bitterness of the water does not taste of God as she swallows it. She has no power over her own body to take or not to take, to drink or not to drink, to tremble or not to tremble. She has not the authority nor the wherewithal to protect her unborn child. Her hair a mess, her face bloated from crying, the woman breaks my heart with her broken acquiescence: "Is it gone? Is it gone? Amen. Amen."

Only the woman and her God know the origin of that piece of her flesh and its innocence. The husband and his priest, the men, have been betrayed by their jealousy. There is, to my mind, no logic to which child lives or dies.

After all is said and done, surely the women will tend to her, reserving their judgment for God and man.

Until the doctor asked me, it had not crossed my mind to blame God for the miscarriage, for all that it did seem unfair. Now I wondered, in a dark, damp nest of prayers, whether God could not in fact have made it work out after all.

■   ■   ■

When Bathsheba told the king that she was pregnant, after his adulterous, covetous, royally abusive use of her, David contrived to lose both mother and child to mundane respectability. He recalled her husband, Uriah, from the battlefield and tried to tempt the man with his own wife. When that didn't work, David schemed to get the man killed (see 2 Sam. 11).

Scripture does not tell us whether David confessed his murderous conspiracy to Bathsheba or whether he simply pretended to be kind, taking her into his home, this widow pregnant with the child he had tried to disown, whom he now took as his own. If she did know about the assassination of Uriah, you may be sure that she kept her knowledge to herself. Whatever David might say, that is not, she knew, how love operates.

Nor does scripture tell us what Bathsheba was doing while David fasted and prayed and wailed and wept, crying out to God for the life of the child he had tried not to love. We weep with David, while Bathsheba is locked out of the story, with the other mothers silenced by the Bible: Sarah, who was not offered an audience to state her case against Abraham's imminent sacrifice of their son (see Gen. 22); the mother of Jephthah's daughter, whose only child was offered to God by the man as the spoils of war (see Judg. 11); Rizpah, silent as the grave, watching over the dead (see 2 Sam. 21); the daughters of Rachel, weeping over their own lost sons, the children of their sorrow, unconsoled under the reign and ruin of Herod's madness (see Matt. 2:16-18).

For a week, David lay before God, pleading the innocence, the brief and empty life of his son. But when he discovered that it was finished, David got up and bathed, changed his clothes, and washed his face, unwilling to argue with God anymore (see 2 Sam. 12:15-23).

Bathsheba, meanwhile, was locked out of the story, wailing with the women, "Is he gone? Is he gone?"

Her hair disheveled and her shame on show for the royal court, she knew that whatever the prophet might say or her husband might pray, a wise and loving God does not prey on the hearts of mothers by way of their wombs or the little ones who die without a name. That does not smack of divine justice. That way madness lies.

■   ■   ■

Three years after they left the house with the duck pond, in another house, filled with the mess of buckets and toys, plastic spoons, and baby pictures, my parents-to-be received a letter, which read:

> We have been offered a baby girl in whom we think you may be interested. . . .
>
> If you would like to have the background details of this baby for consideration, I should be very pleased to send them to you if you would telephone me at this office as soon as possible.
>
> Yours sincerely,
> Organisinf Secretary [sic]

They did not know it, but when my parents began the process of my adoption, my mother was pregnant once

57

more. It was her second and final ectopic pregnancy. I would be her second and final child.

When I discovered my own second pregnancy, I was halfway out of a reactive depression brought on by grief, and halfway up a literal, physical mountain in England's Lake District. I stopped short and announced to my bewildered husband, "I feel strange. I think I'm pregnant. I don't want to go up any farther." We trekked back down to the village with the only pharmacy in that rural region. While my husband chivalrously and in some confusion went in to find me a home pregnancy test, I sat on the edge of the stone village well, that biblical image of fertility and blessing, now serving as a fundraiser for children's charities. Instead of wishes, I made an offering and filled it with my prayers, not for what might happen next but of thanksgiving for what I already knew, the life I was rediscovering, coming to new terms within myself.

Questions for Reflection

- Where have you faced frustration, tragedy, or disappointment in your search for family and its fulfillment? Where was God for you when that happened?
- Who are your sisters, brothers, siblings, or others from scripture in those times of trial? How can their stories help you to heal?

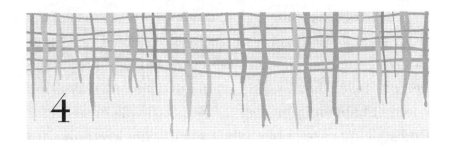

4

Dedication: Samson, Samuel, and Hannah

When my eldest daughter was a baby, I heard a sermon that took parents to task regarding their Christian responsibilities to their children. The preacher's main concern was for parents to take more care when crossing the street with a stroller. He lived, it seemed, in fear of driving around corners where parents rocked their wheels to and fro dangerously close to the curb. The preacher admonished us that our children belonged first to God and were only "on loan" to their earthly parents, to take care of for a while; parents should observe the Green Cross Code or "curb drill" or pedestrian safety rules as closely as any religious ritual. It wasn't bad advice, but it was the loaner language that got to me.

I heard the sermon as I struggled with the loss of my first baby, the one never born. Even as I held her sister in my arms; even though I believed that God had taken her on, taken her in, and completed her in ways that couldn't happen in my womb; even as I was grateful for God's loving care of her, when I could not keep up with her little life, I was seriously ungrateful for her death. Sitting with my firstborn child that morning at church, listening to the preacher talk about her like a library book borrowed from the hallowed halls of heaven, I told God silently, sullenly, *If you want this one back, you'll have to go through me.*

Of course, children are never ours to keep. One of the first ideas that an infant owns is that of a hungry, sleepy, needy, beloved self, which is not its mother or its father or its teddy bear. From the moment they are born and the umbilical cord cut, they begin to grow apart from us. In some ways, the children we keep and see every day are as opaque a mystery as the children we lose sight of, one way or another; as much a marvel and a mystery as the One in whose image they are made.

Our biblical record is littered with miraculous children who are dedicated to their Maker and who remain a puzzle and perplexity to their mothers.

Samson's birth was the result of his mother's encounter with the angel of the Lord. She was minding her own business one day when the stranger arrived out of nowhere and told her to clean up her life, cut out the wine and the unclean foods, for she was to have a son who would live as a *nazirite*, dedicated to God, exempt from strong drink and a haircut. Twice, she told her husband, the strange man appeared and told her the same thing. Her husband, swallowing his pride and his natural suspicion, sought to detain the angel at its second coming with the offer of dinner, to find out just what this stranger might mean by telling his wife she was with child. Only after the angel ascended on the flame of his burnt sacrifice did Manoah realize that the encounter was innocent, awesome, and as terrifying a birth announcement as anyone could receive.

As much as his annunciation and birth were bewildering, Samson must have been a challenge to his parents' understanding: showing up at strange times with wild honey and with or without wild women, whom he may or may not have wed. He was a strange one, Samson, made a mystery from before his conception, before his mother first felt the twinge of misgiving in her digestion; before the misplacement of her first monthly period. Whatever purpose his parents might have thought God had for him, Samson made his own way in life, making a riddle of his life and a mess of his relationships. He could have used a few visiting angels himself (see Judg. 13–16).

■   ■   ■

While the prophet Samuel too was given to God as a *nazirite*, this time, his mother sought out God to make the bargain rather than vice versa (see 1 Sam. 1). I spent plenty of time in prayer bargaining alongside Hannah. Perhaps what follows contains too much projection, but this is how I heard her story as she kept me company in my conversations with God about our children.

Hannah was rich in everything except that which her heart and body desired. Her husband complained, "Am I not enough for you?" He wooed her happiness with double portions of meat and gladness, but Hannah would not be bought, nor her grief paid down. Her husband could not understand it; but then, he had it all. She had nothing, no one, that did not belong to somebody else (see 1 Sam. 1:1-8).

There are those days when, overflowing with the hunger and hormones of abundant humanity, a woman will frighten men and gods alike. Hannah spilled herself into the temple, the fullness of her feminine appetite for life, for love, for satisfaction flowing silently all over the floor and scenting the very air. The priest was justifiably worried. He tried scolding, but she was too far gone, too wide open, too wounded and wound up to be mollified or shamed or shut down (see 1 Sam. 1:9-16).

"There is nothing wrong with me!" she told him; yet, *What is wrong with me?* her soul whispered. *Why will you not give me the child I know you have stolen from my womb, because it feels hollow and haunted without him? Give him back, lend him to me for a little while and I promise I will tell him that he really belongs to you.*

The priest, scandalized and scared, sent Hannah away for God to handle. "Go in peace"? I wonder in what tone of voice that was said (see 1 Sam. 1:17).

After Samuel was born, I rather fancy Hannah regretted the promise to share him. She named him, dutifully, after his origins in her prayer, her petition; but for years afterward she hid him in her bosom, as though God would never find him there. Back and forth Hannah walked in her mind, pacing the floor in the night when he cried with colic, hiding in the halls by day as though God were hiding in the sunlight, waiting to surprise her with her promise: "Hannah! You said he was mine!"

When her husband, Elkanah, went up to Shiloh to offer his annual sacrifice and all his household with him, Hannah hung back, pretending sleep, faking the flu, hugging the child to her breast like a shield. She said, "I will go when I have weaned him." She would not go back to Shiloh, into the presence of God, until she was good and ready, until she had filled her heart and it could hold no more of him. She told God, "You will have him all the days of his life; but for now, he is mine, and

I am keeping him to myself. For now, I am holding him. For now, I am holding on to him" (see 1 Sam. 1:21-23).

And what must Elkanah think? Year by year her husband left, puzzling over her, his devout, devoted wife who now would not darken the doorstep of the temple. She flinched when he asked her to come with him to the feast, as though he were asking her to sacrifice her own child instead of a three-year-old bull. "Not until he is weaned of me," she told him, and her husband practiced his puzzled patience until he could wait no longer (see 1 Sam. 1:21-23).

At length, did he put down his foot: "It is time!"? Otherwise she might never have returned.

Hannah brought Samuel back to Shiloh and handed him over to the priest. Even then, she told Eli, "I have lent him to the LORD" (1 Sam. 1:28). *But indeed*, I heard her whisper once again in silent prayer, *he is mine.*

Hannah let Samuel go, let him grow, piece by piece; first her body releasing his, then her breasts, then her arms, then her needle-pricked fingertips. I feel for Hannah. I can almost see her, holding her sleeping child, her face obscured by a tent of her hair. I recognize her, the tilt of her head, the tired arms unwilling, unable to set the baby down, just yet; swaying gently to the rhythm of love.

From that time forward, this flesh of her flesh, bone of her bone, became a mystery to Hannah. Each year, when the family visited Shiloh, she would bring Samuel a robe that she had made for him (see 1 Sam. 2:18-20). But she would have to guess at how much he had grown, how much bone and flesh he had added, how much weight and heft, how much hair—which must never be touched by razor or flint, because she had lent him to the LORD as a *nazirite* from before his birth.

Hannah had to guess and imagine and dream of him as she had before he was born. She stitched everything that she had missed about him into his new garment, so that when she saw him, it would not be too much of a shock. But he no longer belonged or fit within her bosom.

At the end of his life, Samuel returned to Ramah. "I have lent him to the LORD; as long as he lives, he is given to the LORD," Hannah had promised (1 Sam. 1:28); but in death she would have him home. He was buried in Ramah (see 1 Sam. 25:11). Was it the same Ramah where Hannah had once held him, and held onto him, and refused to let him go, no matter her bargain with the divine, on which she would make good only on her own terms? And it seems, after all, that God knew better than to fight her for him.

■　　■　　■

My own impending birth was not announced by an angel, although it might have caused a similar tremor of terror in my mother. I was intrigued to discover that after my birth, the church had, in a way, been my first foster family, my adoption having been arranged by the Church of England Children's Society.

Twenty-nine years later, I traveled to London with a toddler and a baby in tow to visit the offices that housed the archives of that original adoption agency; somewhere along the way the church label had fallen off, but an aura of grace surrounded the social worker who greeted us. We were hours late; the city was a headache. We were fraught (me), flustered (the toddler), and outright screechy done-with-it-all (the baby). Still, the social worker welcomed us as though this were our homecoming. She was the most maternal presence I think that I had ever encountered in a stranger. In that moment, she was an angel, a messenger of another life, and she shared my history with me in black and white, old photocopies of old papers.

I read the story of being let go, piece by piece, recorded first in old-fashioned handwriting, then typed neatly onto an official form, "Application for the Adoption of a Child." The particulars that made it from the draft to the final document tell of the social worker's discernment of the salient details. The baby's mother is described repeatedly, throughout the file, as "an attractive and intelligent girl." One almost expected to find next a description of her womb as "well-appointed" and her situation as "refreshingly modern."

Between themselves, one social worker to another notes that, "[The mother] has not been to visit [the baby] at the foster home since taking her there, but asks anxiously about her progress, which has been excellent."

My birth mother signs in her schoolgirl hand a cer- tificate, confirming that she has read and understood something titled "Adoption of Children—Explanatory Memorandum."

Hardly a *nazirite*, nevertheless my religious upbring- ing was directly addressed in the intake documents signing me over to the adoption agency's guardianship. According to my records, my mother instructed that I was to be raised in "any Protestant denomination." I believed I heard the practiced phraseology of the social worker behind the written words. My new parents ful- filled the promise, having me christened in the Church of England just as soon as it was legally safe to do so in my brand-new name.

As strange as the story was to read, I was struck by the sudden familiarity of my father's handwrit- ing. The Society had even kept the letter he wrote at Christmastide, detailing my progress in the family.

You will be pleased to know that Rosalind is now very firmly established as a member of our fam- ily and is greatly loved . . .

We are looking forwards to her first Christmas,
though she will in all probability be more interested in the wrappings than what is inside.

A photograph of my baby self accompanied the letter,
photocopied and reserved for decades against the day
that I might return. I would not have known myself
from it.

■   ■   ■

In my attic, there are three dresses set aside against the
possibility, someday, of a child who will fill them. One
is the outfit I wore to court the day I was adopted. The
other two are hand-me-downs from my sisters, the ones
I met when I found my birth mother. She had set these
painstakingly hand-smocked dresses aside in case
of a grandchild. Receiving them from her hands was
about as great an affirmation of her abiding love as I
could imagine. My own daughters have grown into and
grown out of those dresses that my birth mother and
her mother sewed at a time when we did not know one
another's names, and now they wait, for God-knows-
who, to lay claim to them, to us, at least for as long as
love lasts.

In the beginning, or very near to it, after God asked
Adam and Eve who on earth had told them they were

naked, and after seeing the flimsy job they did with their fig-leaf coverings, God sewed clothes for them. What it cost God to skin and clean the creatures whose hides formed the hiding place for shame is not described, although God had only just created them and clothed their own backs with fur. How hard it must have been to choose the raw material for Adam's first coat; yet that is what God did, before they walked out of the Garden and away from the only Father they had ever known.

One day, we are promised, when the children of God finally return from their long exile, like Adam and Eve, we will receive new garments, and the Son of God himself will finish clothing us:

I, Ezra, saw on Mount Zion a great multitude that I could not number, and they all were praising the Lord with songs. In their midst was a young man of great stature, taller than any of the others, and on the head of each of them he placed a crown, but he was more exalted than they. And I was held spellbound. Then I asked an angel, "Who are these, my lord?" He answered and said to me, "These are they who have put off mortal clothing and have put on the immortal, and have confessed the name of God. Now they are being crowned, and receive palms."

(2 Esd. 2:42-45)

■ ■ ■

We do not, I think, borrow our children from God, nor from one another. In my imagination, the call of God on a mother, on Hannah, on Mary, on the rest of us is not to hold our children more lightly—nor more tightly—but to love them more fiercely. I do not understand myself as a deputy to God in mothering to my children but as a stargazer, looking in wonder at the ongoing work of creation standing next to me, awed and frequently perplexed by the heavenly creature that God has sent to live with me. Birth and dedication, labor and loss, creation and sacrifice, all live within the rhythm of God's love. We live with it all, with God, with one another, because our families are ours only insofar as they are ours to love, and love is not relinquished. When it no longer fits the mold we have made for it, love sews a new coat.

Questions for Reflection

■ When have you negotiated with God? What is nonnegotiable?

■ What have you given up for God? What has God given up for you in such negotiations?

■ What patterns of family life have you outgrown? What new webs of relationship have you woven in their place?

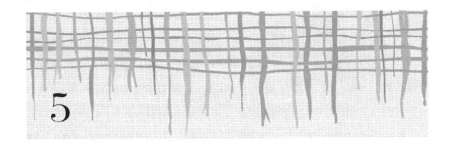

5

Genealogies

There are two kinds of people in the world: the ones who have read *The Lord of the Rings* in its entire, triple glory; and the ones who skipped the elvish saga songs.

I am a skipper. This is my confession.

When my congregation decided to read the Bible in one Christian year, Advent 1 through Christ the King, we found a lot of stories that surprised us; ones that we had either never heard or had forgotten, accidentally or subliminally or on purpose. We also found plenty of parallels to the elvish songs. For some, it was the lists of battles and conquests. For others, it was the fine detail of the buildings, early blueprints. Census data appeal to a particular kind of mind, but not to many others. Still others found the genealogies hypnotic, soporific, skippable.

I was such a skipper. I could try to justify myself citing Timothy, warning people "not to occupy themselves with myths and endless genealogies that promote speculations rather than the divine training that is known by faith" (1 Tim. 1:4); but I confess that in my heart, I understood that he was talking more about *The Da Vinci Code* than about the words of scripture.

But a writer does not generate words to no purpose. Like the songs of the elder folk, these lists and litanies were passed down first by word of mouth, repeated to perfection, polished to a pearl by teeth and tongues spiced by food and fire, loosened by company and community. Before the advent of the printing press, copyists pored over each cubit and gem and generation, preserving details that I have often failed to appreciate, to tell us something important, something that matters, something of the matter of God.

For example, in the beginning, the genealogies read forward, promoting the expansion of creation, the generation and multiplication of relatives and relationships, children of the living God, not reading back down the heaped bones of dead ancestors.

And the genealogies of Jesus (see Matt. 1:1-17; Luke 3:23-38) are hardly a straightforward story. The differences from Matthew to Luke far exceed the similarities. The two evangelists do not even agree on the name of Joseph's father, and from there on back, it is all downhill from a family detective's point of view. They point in opposite directions, forward and backward; they skip or add generations. Luke's purpose is the more transparent: He crafts a tree of life that has its roots in the garden of Eden itself and the fruit of Adam—although Matthew too may nod in that direction, titling his genealogy grandly in Greek, *Book of the Genesis of Jesus Christ* (Matt. 1:1).[1]

There are names that appear only in Matthew. We know nothing else about them other than their place in this list except that they were, presumably, fathers, and sons, and fathers again. Did they fall in love? Were their wives beloved, although unnamed? Did these mystery men marry good mothers and inherit fine sons?

Curiously too, while Matthew claims to have described fourteen generations three times over, his numbers do not add up. So, who is missing from the list? Matthew is infamous for interposing the names of women into a traditionally masculine song; but Matthew, even with all of his fondness for women's names, does not name Bathsheba. Matthew has the gall still to describe her as the wife of Uriah, even after David has killed him and claimed her and grieved the loss of their first child together. So, if Matthew could include the cuckolded Uriah, whose blood was spilled and not passed down the rest of the line at all (see 2 Sam. 11); if Matthew could include Rahab, prostitute and spy (see Josh. 2); if he could include Tamar, who "played the whore" to shame her husband's family for forsaking her, who gave birth to her own husband's twin brothers, sons of the same father (Gen. 38); if Matthew included all of these without blushing, then what unnamable sins are hidden between the unknown names in the final litany of the forefathers of Jesus, the Son of God, who came into the world to save such desolate sinners (see 1 Tim. 1:15)? It simply doesn't add up.

These songs are full of intrigue, sometimes lost, perhaps in translation, waiting for the unwary to be tripped into revelation by the hypnotic lull and lilt of the lists. In the mess of roots beneath the surface of their fancy family trees are hidden sequences of code lying in wait for the curious and observant reader to express their purpose. In the gaps, in the spaces, in the holes hide errant ancestors, responsible for the family secrets, buried alive with their exploits.

■ ■ ■

My own elvish song reads this way: I had joined a national organization for adult adoptees, and they organized a day trip to London, to the General Register Office, a guided tour of the labyrinth of birth, death, and marriage records designed to unravel some meaning from the coded messages of our new and original birth certificates, to find our biological roots. The outing was organized for my birthday, which seemed like a coded message in itself. I thought that I should go. I even signed up, but when the day came, I skipped it. I told myself I was sick, but whether it was sickness of the body or the soul of expectation, I have my doubts. But my husband is a scientist. He enjoys data. He was more than happy to take my failure to launch into London as an opportunity to offer himself as a research assistant. There was, of course, no real need to travel so far. Our county library had all of the records stored on microfiche slides.

One of the advantages of a traditional patriarchy is its standardization of record-keeping. Another is that my mother had married and taken the name of a man with an uncommon surname, making her much easier to track through the records than, for example, Mrs. Smith or Mrs. Jones. By the time he came home from his afternoon excursion, my husband had the home address of my grandparents, the names of a few of my half-siblings, and the location of the house in the south of England where they had been born.

"She likes being a mother," he gently told me, reading a story between the lines.

He had looked through another five years of records without finding another birth certificate from the marriage, so he thought that the family he had found must be complete. He thought he had all the details we might need. But they were no longer living at the address he had uncovered, nor anywhere else in the surrounding jurisdictions.

We needed more data. We ordered the long-form birth certificates of my mother and the youngest child. My half-sibling's birth certificate listed her father's occupation, and inspiration hit. There were a handful of major cities in Britain where someone of his profession might have moved for career advancement. Given his unusual surname, it was easy to check the regional telephone directories. Before the Internet age, this meant my husband thumbing through large volumes in the reference library at work during lunchtime. The man was literally reading the phone book for me. He called me at home one day: "I found them."

My unflappably calm post-adoption social worker checked the electoral rolls for us and confirmed that this was my birth mother's family we had found. "There's another child, though," she told me. My youngest semi-sibling was born just beyond the parameters of my husband's original search. Sometimes it pays to persist with the list, even when we have lost count of the many superfluous details. Who knows what surprises are hiding, buried beyond the limits of hope or (dare we admit it?) boredom?

■ ■ ■

I was convicted and humbled during my church's communal Bible-reading expedition, by the parishioner who told me that his favorite part was the foray into the detailed instructions for building a Temple to God. "Why on earth?" I asked. "Because it shows how much God cares," he replied. Of course, he was right, and his single-sentence sermon folded this preacher's skimming, beat-skipping heart into an origami ornament, pretty, decorative, and flimsy.

But it's funny how the words of a song will stick in the memory even when we are not paying attention. A couple of decades after I skipped the trip to the General Register Office, I was traveling through a different part of London that I didn't know. The street names were strangely familiar, as though I had read them on a map or listed in an atlas; as though they were part of my history, although I knew with some certainty that I had never visited that quarter before.

I took the Tube to the British Library and took tea with my birth mother. "You must have walked past our old house," she told me, and the penny dropped. I was staying around the corner from the address on that old birth certificate, the clue in the long and thready trail of breadcrumbs that led me, eventually, to this café, to sit across the table from a relative stranger whom I had learned, as though in a strange and ancient, newly revived language, to love.

Questions for Reflection

- Have you ever traced your own family history, through genealogies or DNA testing? What surprises did you find?
- How do you relate your biological or cultural family history to the family history of our faith ancestors?

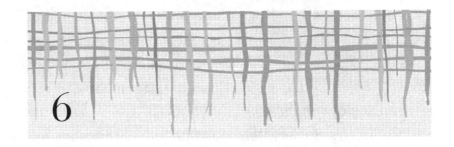

6

Naming and Claiming: Jacob, Naomi, and God

There is a woman in the congregation where I preach named Joy. Whenever I preach a sermon about joy, I have to apologize to her. I know the tug at the center of one's being when one's name is called out or whispered or overheard. She laughs. There could be worse reasons to feel jumpy than a surfeit of joy.

■   ■   ■

When the social worker wrote to my mother, it was in a code that no one else would recognize.

> I am writing on behalf of Caroline, whom you last met back in 1968. She would like to be in touch with you.

Only in that building, anonymous in the heart of London, have I ever heard my old name spoken aloud as though it were mine, as though it meant me. I do not know the words that would describe that feeling.

The social worker, the kind woman who worked for the Children's Society, laid out her plan to contact my birth mother.

"We never know who in the household might open the letter first," she explained. It was clear that what we were doing, breaking into my birth mother's life unannounced, arriving in such an innocent envelope on the doormat, was dangerous, potentially explosive. It was serious business. It had never before occurred to me to be afraid for her.

"We write the letter in such a way that it doesn't give any unnecessary information." If a suspicious husband or an oblivious aunt or a nosy child were to open the letter, it would be puzzling; but my mother would have every chance to make up whatever story she chose to explain it away, should she choose to or should she need to. No one whom she did not trust with her secret would know the name of the baby, Caroline.

"I won't send it until the end of the week," the social worker continued. "We put them in the post last thing on Friday, and we send them second class. That way, there is no chance that the letter will arrive over the weekend, when there's no one here." She would put her name and direct phone number in the letter. When the mail arrived, she wanted to be sure that my birth mother could pick up the phone right away and find someone who knew just what she was talking about, just what it all meant.

"I am writing on behalf of Caroline, whom you last met in 1968. She would like to be in touch with you."

The message was in code, and my hidden, unused birth name was the key.

Those of us in my generation and geographical location were born without names. No one knew before the baby was born whether it would be a girl or a boy, and except in rare instances, names were withheld until the deed was done and the outcome presumed unmistakable. (How presumptuous we human parents can be.)

My birth mother gave me "a good, English name with no baggage," as she described it when we met, which I interpreted to mean that no one in the family would object to my taking it away with me. I did not know I had borne that name until I was a teenager. It had never occurred to me to ask. When I did ask, my parents readily shared what little information they had. I was given two names to be going on with: a beginning and a middle, Caroline Anne; no last name. Those seemed innocuous. I could have lived with them. My mother—Ann, the one who raised me—enjoyed that my middle name, Anne, was only one letter away from her own.

Strangely, when I came to claim my birth certificate, it also gave me two names: a first name and a family name. The middle name of which my mother was so fond was missing. It turned out that Anne was the name of my birth mother. The social worker suggested that someone in the process had tried to pass on a clue by tagging me with her name, a secret message about the identity of my first mother, a trail of breadcrumbs to find a way back, if I ever heard the call.

But my parents did not keep any of our birth names; they gave me one out of a Shakespeare comedy. At least it wasn't a tragedy.

Now, in the writing of a coded letter, my unused name had taken on sudden significance, a gravitas it had never before commanded. It was such an ordinary name to bear such weight.

But since we were reintroduced, my birth mother has always used the same name for me that everyone else does. It is as though that other name belongs to another me, a child from a parallel universe, full of infinite possibilities, one whom I barely know.

■　■　■

There is an inherent power differential in the choosing of names. Parents name their children; the children do not generally get a choice in the matter.

A name can be given as a threat. The prophet Hosea's daughter is named *Lo-ruhamah*, "Not pitied," as a warning from God. Her younger brother is named *Lo-ammi*, "Not my people," "for you are not my people and I am not your God" (Hos. 1:9). This from the God who is steadfast in faithfulness and loving-kindness.

A name can be redeemed as a promise. *Lo-ammi* becomes *Ammi*, "My people." *Lo-ruhamah* becomes *Ruhamah*, when God takes pity upon her (see Hos. 2:1).

Almost every name given in the Bible is given a meaning, from Adam, the earthling, and Eve, the lively one, through Moses, drawn out of the waters, and Samuel, God's answer to prayer. From the Creation onward, there are instances of naming and renaming throughout the Bible. We get lists and lists of genealogy. Writing the birth of Jesus, Matthew finds it instructive to trace his ancestry back through a long litany of names all the way to Abraham. Luke goes further, all the way back to Adam, all the way back to God.

God is coy about God's own name, refusing to reveal it to Jacob, God's own Israel, reluctantly revealing it to Moses.

God said to Moses, "I AM WHO I AM.". . .
God also spoke to Moses and said to him: "I am the LORD. I appeared to Abraham, Isaac, and

Jacob as God Almighty, but by my name 'The
LORD' I did not make myself known to them."

(Exod. 3:14, 6:2-3)

God's reluctance to make a name for Godself has been
followed by our own reluctance to pronounce the unpro-
nounceable, the untranslatable, the unspeakable; to
name God as anything other than what God is: God; or by
a multitude of descriptive nicknames: Almighty, Mother-
Father, Creator, Redeemer, Sustainer, Wisdom, Word.

I will admit to some trepidation when I visited the
banks of the Jabbok in the Kingdom of Jordan. It was
our first day in the country, and when our minibus
pulled up by the side of the road, we seemed to be in
the middle of nowhere. There was nothing to see but a
stream, caught between the steep cliffs of a deep gully,
and our own little caravan of weary travelers, jet-lagged
and short on sleep and understanding.

"This is Jabbok," we were told, "where Jacob crossed
over."

What had seemed an innocent stream took on a current of danger. There was a part of me, as I took off my
shoes to approach the riverbed, muscles that stiffened
in warning, asking, "Are you sure you want to go there?"

We stood a while in the narrow valley, in the cool
water, trying to imagine driving a caravan of camels,
sheep, goats, servants, children, wives, provisions, the

spoils of a back-and-forth, cat-and-mouse, dog-eat-dog relationship with Laban, Jacob's double-edged father-in-law, up through the ford and over the blind hill on the other side.

Jacob sent his family on ahead and waited by the ford for the courage to face his brother, his twin, the part of himself he had left behind when he fled his home with his father's blessing and his mother's ambition and his brother's shame as his shield and his provision. All night, he wrestled with himself, with God, with a stranger who would not let him go.

"What is your name?" asked the stranger.

And he said, "Jacob." Then the man said, "You shall no longer be called Jacob, but Israel, for you have striven with God and with humans, and have prevailed" (Gen. 32:27-28).

Prevailing meaning simply to survive, it seems, in such circumstances, since God calls Israel, but when Jacob asks for the name of his wrestling partner, he is met with incredulity and left with a dislocated hip to haul up the hillside toward his brother, his home.

There is power in the choosing and the using of a name; and there is power in its withholding.

Naomi chose her own name. Naomi, in the book of Ruth, returned to Bethlehem, with her daughter-in-law Ruth in tow, two widows alone in the world, robbed by famine and pestilence of their husbands, Naomi's sons,

Ruth's home, and her gods. When she returned, it is little wonder that Naomi tried not to bring back with her the name with which she left.

> When they came to Bethlehem, the whole town was stirred because of them; and the women said, "Is this Naomi?" She said to them,
>
> "Call me no longer Naomi,
> call me Mara,
> for the Almighty has dealt bitterly with me.
> I went away full,
> but the LORD has brought me back empty;
> why call me Naomi
> when the LORD has dealt harshly with me,
> and the Almighty has brought calamity upon
>   me?"
>
> (Ruth 1:19-21)

Naomi means "pleasant," and *Mara*, "the bitter one," was not feeling too pleasant by the time she got back to Bethlehem. It is a difficult way to get there, but these two women—Ruth, who chose for herself her family, her faith, her country; and Naomi, who chose her own name—each of them found through the stripping away of all that had held them in their assigned places the freedom to choose who they would be. Mara's naming of herself is a brave display of her nakedness before the people who would clothe her in widow's weeds, paint her safely back into her corner of the world: Naomi, who never gave any trouble.

Even so, everyone still called her Naomi.

Some names stick. Others are rescinded. Still others were meant only for special occasions or special relationships. Despite the dramatic and divine aspects of his renaming ceremony in the river, even Israel by the very next sentence is back to being called Jacob. Israel seems to hover somewhere on the borders of the holy; safer to continue to use Jacob for everyday and family planning. Israel appears in the psalms, on cultic occasions, and in ritual language. Jacob, in the meantime, is the one who limps back towards his brother, so long ago slighted and cast aside, so close in the womb, now an unpredictable stranger, dangerous, holding half of Jacob's identity in his hands with the reins of his camel and the hem of his robe.

■　　■　　■

My friend Evan changed his name as he began to live publicly into his identity as a man.

Evan's first name change came about because of difficult family circumstances. An abusive and eventually absent father gave way to a stepfather who loved and cared for Evan as his own. He was unable legally to adopt the child, so upon the attainment of majority age, Evan adopted him, going through a legal process to take his last name, sending a birth announcement to the new parents that his mother and stepfather had become. Now, everyone would know that they belonged together, as a family.

Later in life, it was harder to shed the family attachments of the first name he had borne since birth, which had belonged to one whom his mother and her family had loved even before his birth.

When Evan's mother was pregnant with him, her brother's family was also expecting a baby. These siblings had lost a sister, and each wanted to name their new baby after her. The parents agreed that whoever was born first would win the family name. Evan won the race out of the womb and was rewarded with the name of his lost aunt. His mother added her own middle name, another family connection.

When the time came to change his name to one that better reflected the man into whom he had grown, Evan pondered for a moment keeping his late aunt's name. It would be unusual, but not unheard of for a man. He decided it could be too confusing for those who might already be confused by his changing appearance and presentation. I asked about his mother's middle name; my own youngest child has my middle name as her own. That would be hard for me to let go. Evan uses the initial. He and his mother both signed their names that way anyway, he said.

The day after the legal ceremony to stamp his name change as official, Evan preached a service at the church he serves as parish priest. A friend led prayers and renewed the promises of baptism, using Evan's new name. Evan preached about the importance of becoming whom we are called to be by God and how that becoming can be a lifetime's journey.

Of course, his original baptismal certificate, his ordination certificates, his seminary degree, all bear a dead name. There are even those who use his old name as a stick with which to try to nudge him back into the lane they have defined for him; to keep him in his place in their imagination. He is working with people within the church to recognize the need for that community to honor what God already knows: that Evan was Evan before he was baptized, ordained, sent out into the world of ministry to encourage others to find out what wonders of life God has in store for them. He is using the power of his name, his chosen name, the one by which God knows him, to reshape the world around him.

Questions for Reflection

- Were you named for someone in your family history? How did you come by your name?
- By what name does God know you? Is it the same name that everyone else uses or is it a different one?
- By what name(s) do you know God? Does it make a difference to your faith or your prayer which name you use?

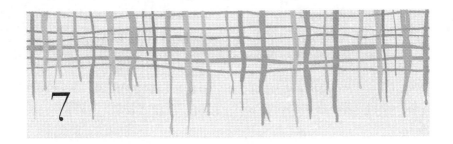

Family Politics:
Moses

Scripture does not describe Pharaoh's family in detail. We know that he had a daughter. We know that his firstborn died. As Wilda C. Gafney points out in her *Womanist Midrash*, we do not know whether the princess and the doomed firstborn child were the same person.[1] My reading of Moses' birth and backstory has been changed up by Gafney's take on the princess's brief appearance in our scriptures.[2] She notes that we do not know how it came about that Pharaoh's daughter was permitted to adopt a child whom her father had condemned to die, whose life he considered of less worth than that of a fly. Gafney reads the princess as "an ally of the Hebrew people";[3] the young woman might also have been motivated by the opportunity to troll her own father. So much remains unsaid in the great book of Exodus; but we who have families, and political opinions, might imagine the kinds of conversation that took place over the dinner tables of the elite and the oppressed in the time of an unkind pharaoh.

■　■　■

Pharaoh commanded all his people, "Every boy that is born to the Hebrews you shall throw into the Nile, but you shall let every girl live."

(Exod. 1:22)

At dinner that night in the Pharaoh family, an argument was rehearsed that was, to the father's ears, already becoming old.

"But, Dad, how could you?"

"Now look, my pet, you have a warm heart, but it is a woman's heart. And after all, aren't I letting the women live and breed and have their daughters learn the lullabies of their people, as women are supposed to do?"

The pharaoh smiled indulgently at his daughter, and he broke off another piece of bread to dip into his hummus and point sloppily across the table, softly, to drive home his point.

"Isn't it because I love you, my daughter, so much, that I let their daughters live?"

The son's chair leg screamed at the floor as he shifted in his seat. The father ignored him, avoided the eye of the mother, and fixed his loving gaze only on his girl-child, his darling, his one hope of an ally among a room full of Hebrew servers and slaves.

"I'm not hungry," she declared importantly and left the table, her own Hebrew handmaid hurrying behind her with her plate of *dolmades* and tomatoes.

Casting about for an audience, the pharaoh finally faced his son.

"I'm not hungry either." The youth attempted dignity, assembling his gangly limbs to stride from the room.

The pharaoh still could not look their mother in the eye.

■　■　■

Now a man from the house of Levi went and married a Levite woman. The woman conceived and bore a son; and when she saw that he was a fine baby, she hid him three months. When she could hide him no longer she got a papyrus basket for him, and plastered it with bitumen and pitch; she put the child in it and placed it among the reeds on the bank of the river. His sister stood at a distance, to see what would happen to him.

(Exod. 2:1-4)

The conversation overheard during dinner at Miriam's home was less politically divided but just as disagreeable as the one at Pharaoh's table. Her mother, worn and wan from night feeds and worry, was snappish and short with Miriam's father, who, weary from the day's labor, had little energy left to squander on the fear that the neighbors might hear the baby and give them away.

"Can't you do something with him?" he demanded testily as the little one started once again to wind up to a wail.

Miriam scurried to pick him up, anxious to keep the peace between her parents. With so much violence in her world, she was zealous to find safe haven for her family between these walls.

It was Miriam's idea to set the baby afloat upstream of the princess's garden. She had heard about the young woman's pity for Miriam's people. She knew that the pharaoh's daughter read the secret papyrus pamphlets that underground agents distributed among the Hebrew women, offering advice on how to hide a baby or its gender and where and when to smuggle it out of the city to safety. As in so many times of tribulation and trial, women who would give their lives for their children made sure instead to live for them. They set up networks and nurseries, dodging the death-dealers and loving their sons hard.

One of the pamphlets gave detailed and illustrated instructions on how to construct a basket for a baby who was just getting old enough to be a danger to itself. There was a brief window of opportunity, between the earliest days of infancy and the time when the child might suddenly learn to roll itself into the river,[4] when a baby boy might with some kind of safety be set afloat, catching the currents below the Hebrews' workplaces and drifting downstream to the waiting women in a community outside of the pharaoh's imagination.

At a river beach below the city, the dark shawl of a weeping woman might catch the glint of a bare, new moon as a tear caught on the fabric and a slight splash and ripple was lost to the river and the night. No one was foolish enough to float their babies by day, when they might waken and cry, nor through the city, where anyone could see them. If they were found, then not only that child's life would be forfeit, but the whole game would be up, and the river would become stagnant, unable to render any hope of life.

But Miriam was not willing to let her little brother out of her sight. She persuaded her mother to let her take charge of his embarkation and launching. All night, she curled around his little basket-casket, praying to the God of her father, of Abraham, Isaac, and Jacob; the God of tricksters. She appealed to the memory of Joseph, who was adopted by the royal house of Egypt once before. In the morning, as the streets were gathering shadows in the lee of the rising sun, they slipped through the public section of the palace gardens, as close as they could come to the princess's place, and when they heard the women laughing, Miriam pinched her brother hard and kissed him desperately, as she and their mother set him afloat.

> The daughter of Pharaoh came down to bathe at the river, while her attendants walked beside the river. She saw the basket among the reeds and sent her maid to bring it. When she opened it, she saw the child. He was crying, and she took pity on him. "This must be one of the Hebrews' children," she said. Then his sister said to Pharaoh's daughter, "Shall I go and get you a nurse from the Hebrew women to nurse the child for you?" Pharaoh's daughter said to her, "Yes." So the girl went and called the child's mother. Pharaoh's daughter said to her, "Take this child and nurse it for me, and I will give you your wages." So the woman took the child and nursed it. When the child grew up, she brought him to Pharaoh's daughter, and she took him as her son. She named him Moses, "because," she said, "I drew him out of the water."
>
> (Exod. 2:5-10)

■ ■ ■

Family politics can be tricky. Even in our own families, hidden rocks and eddies threaten to undermine the love that binds us together. Topics to avoid at the dinner table might include elections, religion, taxes, access to public bathrooms, access to marriage rites, access to Twitter, political appointments, personal safety, personal pronouns, painkillers, prescription prices, medical provision, insurance, indolence, indoctrination. The power dynamics of parent and child, birth parent, grandparent, godparent; the intersecting and extrapolating cycles of influence and affection, pressure and oppression, denial and deviousness should have been enough by themselves to sink the little boat in which Moses floated downstream. The princess might have been moved as much by defiance of her father as compassion for the baby in the bulrushes. She may have developed a hero complex, raised in a household ringed with violence and rumors of violence. She may have hoped by saving one child to save the world. From the Bible, we hear nothing of the table conversation at the next night's dinner, nor how the princess explained the sudden advent of a new and taboo grandchild to her father and mother.

So, Moses lived in two worlds. Hidden, offered to the waters of creation and fate; drawn out, returned, raised, reclaimed; it can only have been confusing for the young child.

Moses not only lived in two worlds, but he lived at the extremes of opposing worlds. He was born into murder and mayhem, hidden away, pretending to be unborn for as long as the trick could be managed. Set adrift on the holy river (because all water is holy) in a rude basket, bitumen pitched by his desperate and hopeful mother and sister, made more for miracles than for beauty, at an unconscionably young age he navigated obstacles: rocks, frogs, and ducks. Woven into a cotton blanket, undyed, he was too big to be swaddled, and his toes got wet.

Moses could pass for an Egyptian, but for his early months and years at his birth mother's breast, hearing his sister's songs and stories; the DNA of his soul was Hebrew. He looked like a slave and dressed like a prince, in soft robes and gold rings, every obstacle swept from his path. He spoke with two tongues, neither totally convincing (see Exod. 4:10; 6:12, 30). At its crisis, his confusion erupted in death, the cycle of his life coming full circle (see Exod. 2:11-15).

In the fairytale version, Moses should be the son of the princess, adopted into the household of the Hebrew slaves, to be redeemed at a later date by a chance encounter and a hidden sign of his royal blood. Instead, he was adopted by the princess, then returned to his mother, only to be taken away again when he had drunk his fill of her milk and motherhood. Everything about his story has become confused and complicated by the strange interplay of the princess and the peasant mother, herself descended from the princes of the Bible; between the pharaoh and the death squads, the slaves and their fearful captors, and the upsetting disorder of the fairytale ending. (God specializes in that.)

It is impossible, anymore, to read Moses' story anyway in the innocent manner of a children's tale. Of course, some communities never had the privilege of removing themselves from the danger of drowning to see only the romance of the river. Now, we are all witnesses to forced family separation; to the desperation of parents who would float their children across borders; and some sink, and some swim, and some are adopted by Egyptian princesses, and some find their way home; and there seems to be no rhyme or reason why one should find a fairytale ending, but almost no one lives happily ever after. Now, while black mothers describe the faith that it takes to send their sons to school or across the street; now, when anti-Semitism, the pharaoh's plague, continues after so many centuries to kill the Hebrew children, even in a new promised land; now, we cannot pretend that the Moses basket is a pretty thing or innocent.

■　■　■

To the end, Moses remains an outsider. That he named his firstborn *Gershom*, "for he said, 'I have been an alien residing in a foreign land,'" is poignant (Exod. 2:22). To which land was Moses foreign—to Egypt or to Midian or to them all? He is given no future in the Promised Land.

Moses burns more bridges than there are in Manhattan between himself and the house of the pharaoh; but his name stays the same. The name given to him by Pharaoh's daughter, "'Because,' she said, 'I drew him out of the water'" (a whole world is hidden in the depths of those waters); that name, the echo and foreshadowing of his rescue from the waters of chaos and death, his history, his heritage; that name remains his own, through thick and thin, hell or high water. God does not give him another when he is adopted again by way of a burning bush.

Moses' relationship with his birth family people remains ironic. After years of travail and trudging, he demands of God,

> "Did I conceive all this people? Did I give birth to them, that you should say to me, 'Carry them in your bosom, as a nurse carries a sucking child, to the land that you promised on oath to their ancestors?'"
>
> (Num. 11:12)

Even for all of this pathos, we do not remember Moses mostly as a fish out of water or as a man out of place, even in the wilderness. We do not remember him as a waif or stray; we do not remember, we tend to forget the young man fearful by night that even God is out for his blood (see Exod. 4:24).

When we remember Moses, we think of greatness; of a man who stood before the pharaoh as an angel of the Lord, a messenger of fearful power. We remember him rustling his people by the thousands through the wilderness, drawing them out of the waters of the Red Sea, cradling them safely in the promises of God. We know him as a prophet on the mountaintop, especially appointed, with behind-the-veil privileges; chosen to receive the name of God.

God followed the lost lamb and set fire to Moses' sorrow. God repurposed the powerful emotions of unbelonging and exile, of complicated love and confusing family ties, politics and the warring positions they set up between factions and family members. In the fairytale that God tells, Moses was born into royalty, a child of the living God, adopted by the warring factions and families of the world and thrown into confusion, only to have his origins revealed in dramatic fashion by the unconsuming fire of the living flame, the spark of life, the spirit of our adoption, which is the redemption of our origins as children of the God who is the first father, nurse, and pharaoh of us all; no exceptions.[5]

Questions for Reflection

- What topics might be considered taboo in your family?
- What topics, if any, do you hold to be taboo in your prayer conversations with God?
- What divides you from Christ and from your neighbor?
- What bridges can you build to help heal those divisions? Who can help you with that?

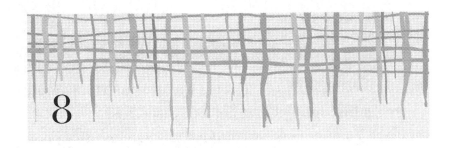

8

Family
and Other Animals

Not every family member is human or divine.

The prophet Nathan tells a parable in which a man loves a lamb like his daughter, feeding it from his table and lavishing affection upon it, and the king is unsurprised (see 2 Sam. 12:1-6). Balaam has a silent-partner relationship with his donkey in the family prophet business, until it finally breaks out, braying at the injustice of Balaam's direction. In fact, the donkey is closer to the messages and messengers of God than Balaam is (see Num. 22:21-35).

Dogs, likewise, are allowed to eat crumbs from the floor beneath the children's table, in Jesus' time as now, and were probably encouraged to do so to save on sweeping up and prevent cockroach infestations (see Mark 7:24-30). The dogs of Egypt obey the Lord in keeping silent as the children of Israel flee on the night of the Passover (see Exod. 11:7). They are instruments of anger against Jezebel and her body (see 1 Kings 21:23); they are companions of comfort to Lazarus, the poor man of the parable reported in Luke who lives outside the rich man's gates (see Luke 16:19-31), as still they serve as faithful companions to those who line the walls outside the habitations and workplaces of the homed and the healthy.

I live with cats. It is disturbing, therefore, to find that there is a significant dearth of cats in the Bible, especially when they are otherwise, in human culture, ubiquitous.

Do you remember that moment in childhood when the Sunday school rote lesson "God is everywhere" became suddenly real and tangible? That moment descending the basement stairs in thick thunderstorm darkness and knowing that the electrically charged air was far from empty? Or the flicker of a candle during dinnertime grace—the subtle movement of the Spirit? The loneliness of a playground fight and the warm, righteous feeling behind your flushed cheeks, behind your hot eyes, that Someone, after all, had your back?

When children grasp for the first time really that God is everywhere, they may ask some strange and seemingly sacrilegious questions in their quest for the truth of God's reach and range:

"Is God in the toilet?"
"Is God on the moon?"
"Is God in my broccoli?"
"Does that mean God is in my tummy now?"

The cat answers all of these questions with a silent and authoritative, "Yes," because the cat (and his hair) also tends to get everywhere, and he has seen God out of the corner of his good eye, evasive as a small, brown mouse, but known, sensed to be ever-present, and by faith believed to be never quite out of reach.

The cat has made it his mission to convey that omni-presence of God, to answer the child's question, by his own feline ubiquity. He has colonized every continent of the earth, even wheedling his way to Antarctica, where he would not let the humans shiver alone on a cold night, nor wonder alone at the everlasting day.

A pilgrim kitten accompanied my journey in Jordan one day. In the early morning, as the sun belabored its rising behind the hill, before the rest of the world was awake, I crept out of the Siq and was confronted by the astonishing rock-hewn façade of the Treasury, left behind long ago by the Nabataeans of Petra. A child of this century, I squatted down to take a photo and was instantly, instantaneously taken over by a small creature distributing red paw prints, dust to dust, over my shorts, lying down on my leg. Playful and pervasive, the small ginger cats looked as though they were put together out of the red rock itself and might in a moment dissolve into the sand.

The humble housecat has domesticated the earth so entirely that there is no escape from her influence, nor from her evangelism on behalf of the omnipresent Lion-tamer.

So, if cats are ubiquitous, where were the felines laying their fur into the purple fabric of Lydia and her friends? Where the almond eyes watching the pigeon seller in the Temple courtyard, catching feathers and pouncing upon shadows as the pigeons pecked about their pens? When Joseph was in prison, did the jailor's cat caterwaul outside his window by night? When Pharaoh's daughter pulled Moses from the River Nile, who pushed the royal cat out of his cradle? There must have been a cat in Gilead, to soothe the troubled soul; a mouser in Bethany; a fisher-cat in Galilee; but according to my secondhand bookstore copy of *Strong's Exhaustive Concordance*, the word *cat* does not crop up even once in the course of a regular reading of the Bible. Instead, *Strong's* jumps directly from *Castor* to *catch*, thence to *caterpillar*.[1] While caterpillars can on occasion be cute and fluffy, this does not make up for the startling omission of cats.

It could, of course, be the case that the Holy Spirit, favoring the form of a dove, had an embargo on cats coming too close. But there was clearly no problem with Noah recruiting lynxes, leopards, and lions for the ark. If there was room for all there, how much more room for our other family members in the mansions of God's household? Perhaps cats (and some other animals) simply do not need the level of scriptural instruction that the rest of the family does.

While the proud Persian and the sapient Siamese do not appear in the regular canon, there are cats in the apocryphal Letter of Jeremiah, included in some Bibles as the sixth chapter of Baruch. Along with some bats and swallows and other birds, the cats sit on the heads and tread on the bodies of graven images and idols. "From this," says Jeremiah, "you will know that [the idols] are not gods; so do not fear them" (The Letter of Jeremiah / Baruch 6:22-23).

The cats know idolatry when they see it and can tell it apart from the real deal (allegedly, they were its objects in Egypt); and they may use their superior wisdom to calm our fears and comfort our anxieties, revealing the warmth of the true God, as well as God's constancy, ubiquity, and famous ineffability.

Questions for Reflection

- What place do nonhuman family members have in your household?
- What do they teach you about the many rooms of heaven?
- Whether or not you live among animals at home, what does the human family's stewardship of the domestic and wild beasts (see Gen. 1:26-28) demand of you?

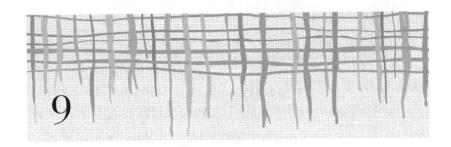

9

Fatherhood: Joseph, Jesus, and God

Joseph, we are given to understand, was a carpenter. He was a man who worked with wood, the great husks of the great creatures that feed us, breathe over us, shelter and shade us. Like a butcher who uses the whole beast, he knew how to honor the carcass of a tree. He was a man who could count the rings and wonder at the wisdom of age. He knew how to highlight a warm beauty; to smooth out the grain as though unfurrowing a creased brow; to bring a peaceful appearance out of the trauma of death, turn loss into a gift.

When Joseph heard about Mary's delicate situation, he was "minded to put her away privily" (Matt. 1:19, KJV). He had no desire toward destruction for the sake of ugliness. He was well chosen, this wooden character,

barely described, left to our biblically informed imagination, to play father to the Son of God.

At night, he would dream. Joseph would surely
have heard of the dryads, the spirits of the oak trees,
but he had no need for such stories when his own bed
sprouted a forest of fluttering paper, messages of God
on white parchment, winged calligraphy, fearsome and
faceless. In a dream, he picked up the letter and read,

> "Joseph, son of David, do not be afraid to take
> Mary as your wife, for the child conceived in her
> is from the Holy Spirit. She will bear a son, and
> you are to name him Jesus, for he will save his
> people from their sins."
>
> (Matt. 1:20-21)

Joseph woke up, his face white and shining with sweat,
lips parted in astonishment. For a moment he looked, if
he only knew it, like an angel.

■   ■   ■

When strangers would say I looked just like my father,
he would beam; I would be embarrassed for them. I
did not know what to think about their misconception
of my conception. In the records of my birth and adoption, my biological father's name is ambiguous. My

birth certificate is fatherless. The adoption society had a name for him, along with some general particulars, designed to reassure prospective adoptive parents that there was nothing to fear from his shadowy presence deep in the child's backstory. My mother was minded to put him away quietly. In any case, instead of him, passersby saw the man at my side and considered how similar we had grown, how he had shaped me and put his imprint upon me.

In the beginning, John describes Jesus as the "son of Joseph from Nazareth" (John 1:45). Both Matthew and Luke trace Jesus' ancestry, by means of different lists and for different reasons, through the man Joseph (see Matt. 1:16; Luke 3:23). His friends and neighbors were convinced, when they saw Jesus, that they saw behind his brow, and in the downsweep of his arm, his mannerisms, heard in his accent echoes of his father, Joseph, the carpenter from Nazareth. They thought that he had done his father proud.

> All spoke well of him and were amazed at the gracious words that came from his mouth. They said, "Is not this Joseph's son?"
>
> (Luke 4:22)

If they remembered that story from his youth, told by friends and family when Mary's back was turned and

Joseph's ears plugged by contentment, then they didn't let on.

The decision that Joseph made was not once for all time. He had to choose them over and again, Mary and the child, over simplicity, respectability, the bliss of ignorance. Sometimes he still dreamed of angels, chasing him to Egypt, luring him home. Each time, he had to wonder anew whether to believe the imaginings of his spirit at night or whether the sensible thing would be to cut and run. Each time, he landed on the side of the angels.

Every child, as he grows, will test the bonds between parent and child, father and son.

It was said to have happened when Jesus was around twelve years old. There was a concerted effort from the town to get down to Jerusalem for the festival. Jesus moved easily between the caravans of mothers, children, and men. He could choose, when his feet blistered and burst, the unsympathetic empathy of his uncles, bent on toughening him up for the rigors of life to come, or the soothing of his mother, who knew how soft and unbroken, how hairless his childish skin still was, although even she was developing a tendency to ask him to lead, to be an example of bravery to the younger children in tow.

It was easy, at that age, for him to get lost.

It is a parent's nightmare. It starts small: an innocent question, "Where is he?" Already, as the words are spoken, there is a rumbling in the pit of the stomach, a rolling realization that this is not the right question, that its utterance already reveals that something is wrong. There is an attempt, at first, to restrain the panic rising, to be reasonable, rational: "Someone must have seen him. Perhaps he is hiding." There is the temptation to cast blame: Strong words are hurled as though in lieu of the sickness that threatens to pour out of a mother's mouth. Even surrender does not bring relief, as it demands that they pull themselves together, together travel back, take back the wounds that have already barbed their skin, their flesh once united by him and now undone. It wasn't even his flesh that united them, and now he is pulling away.

When they found him, Joseph did not trust himself to speak. It was Jesus' mother who brought him back to earth, put him in his place, scolded him like a child: "Your father and I were worried sick! What were you thinking?"

He answered, "Did you not know that I must be in my Father's house?" (Luke 2:49).

And even so, Joseph took them home with him, cursing the choirs of angels singing fight songs in his head (see Luke 2:41-51).

Jesus ran away again, at the age of thirty. This time no one came looking for him, after three days, after forty. Cut loose from the caravan, he was hungry. Satan offered to adopt him, but it was his father's better angels that he summoned to minister to him (see Matt. 4:1-11).

■   ■   ■

My friend Jon, who is himself familiar with fatherhood in its many dimensions, describes Jesus' purpose, in part, to be a search for his original Father. We search with him, asking among the crowd, "Where is your Father?" (John 8:19).

"Whoever has seen me has seen the Father," Jesus told his disciples (John 14:9).

When our son was young, he went through a period of months—a soccer season—during which time he insisted that I be the one to take him to his soccer games, even when his father was home, even when I was tired or busy, even so. Refusal or attempts at redirection would lead to massive meltdowns. It was guilt-inducing for me, most dispiriting for his father, and quite beyond reason. One day, when the issue was not live, I asked our son to try to help me understand.

"It's easier to concentrate when you're there," he explained, "When you take me, I can just ignore you. When Dad comes, I am distracted because I keep wondering what it's like to be a father, sitting in the stands, watching your son play soccer, providing for your family, traveling away from them, coming back . . ."

The strength of identification between a son and his father was something I had never considered, let alone experienced. My son's description of the searching involved, the distraction, the absorption that could interfere even with the attention needed to stop a soccer ball coming at one's head closely followed by a ten-ton teammate (my son played goalkeeper), which would seem pretty basic and instinctual in itself; that commentary, and my conversation with Jon, changed my reading of Jesus' words, as well as my understanding of my son's strong emotions around getting into the car with the wrong parent. It had never occurred to me before that in these moments with his disciples, Jesus was not simply acting theological or biblical, weighty or professorial; he was being human. He was being a man. A glimpse into the world of fathers and sons added, for me, a whole dimension of pathos to Jesus' asides throughout the Gospel of John:

"Father, I thank you for having heard me. I knew that you always hear me, but I have said this for the sake of the crowd standing here."

(John 11:41-42)

"Whoever hates me hates my Father also."
(John 15:23)

"The hour is coming, indeed it has come, when you will be scattered, each one to his home, and you will leave me alone. Yet I am not alone because the Father is with me."
(John 16:32)

"Whoever has seen me has seen the Father."
(John 14:9)

Jesus must have loved Joseph, each man being who he was. And surely it was Joseph whom Jesus was remembering when he told stories of fathers tucked up tightly with their children in bed, even the kindest of them reluctant to leave the warm, soft bodies of their infants, whose limbs swaddled their parents, to answer the door to an importuning friend (see Luke 11:5-9). It was Joseph whom he trusted not to give him a serpentine eel for a fish or a scorpion's nest for an egg (see Luke 11:11-12), even when the boy Jesus did try his temper, ditch his parents, and run off to the Temple.

Still, Jesus longed for the love and for the sight of his heavenly Father, because his identification with God was so complete, so enveloping, so formative that it eclipsed his own will. As close as a thought to its utterance; inspiration to imagination; idea to word, the One in whose image Jesus was born and formed and pre-imagined; the One whom Jesus found so thoroughly and identified with so firmly that he was able to declare,

"If you know me, you will know my Father also. From now on you do know him and have seen him."

(John 14:7)

Questions for Reflection

- How does Jesus' identification of God as his Father resonate with you? Does he expand, confirm, or redeem the idea of fatherhood for you?
- What decisions does God make daily to confirm God's commitment to you, God's child?

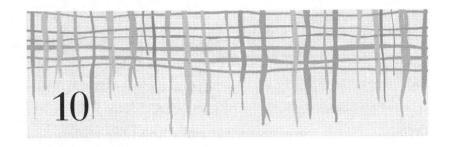

10

Motherhood:
Mary and God

The Queen of Heaven, God-bearer, Madonna. She is the patron saint of women who find themselves standing in front of the bathroom mirror, demanding of its shimmering hard, silvery light, "How can this be? Holy Mary, Mother of God, pray for us now and at the hour of our birth."

Before she became Queen of Heaven, she was just a young girl, surprised to find herself in a situation of dangerous ambiguity.

Medieval artists find her reading by an open window or sewing or praying when the angel catches her unawares, always domestic and domesticated, meek, mild, and unreproachable. Cynics set her to work in the fields, one shawled woman among the wheat sheaves,

119

each as bowed as the other, each one factory-farmed and freedom-free. For all her presumed youth and tenderness, none seem to find her running barefoot from her chores, sneaking comfort from a cool stream, hiding in the shadows of an olive grove, tasting its salty, forbidden fruit; protecting her childhood for as long as she is able, before she is married to domestication and its savory delights.

She was perplexed, the Gospeler tells us, by the angel's appearance (see Luke 1:29); as though perplexity were a reasonable response to such an interruption to the turning of the planet on its axis and the cycle of blood through a young woman's body. Perplexed: a suitable, restrained reaction. Hardly realistic.

Each time I have found myself expecting a child, there has been some perplexity involved. A twinge of confusion, of bodily misdirection, as though something were off-kilter, altered. A sudden cramping calf while crossing the street; I thought, *That's funny. Pregnant legs do that.* By the time confirmation comes, is even sought, the reason for such perplexity is already growing in complexity and causing all kinds of other physical, psychological, and spiritual symptoms.

Mary knew, deep in her spirit and deep in her abdomen, that her body now hovered over holy waters; that she was as one with the Spirit of creation; adopted, married into the family of God, pregnant with possibility.

Somehow, for all her fear and trembling, her "How can this be?"—Mary knew that the angel told the truth. And for all of her bravado, her "Let it be unto me," she was terrified. Following the angel's heavy hint ("By the way, you know your cousin Elizabeth? I was talking to her husband just the other day . . ."), Mary ran for the hills.

> In those days Mary set out and went with haste to a Judean town in the hill country, where she entered the house of Zechariah and greeted Elizabeth.
>
> (Luke 1:39-40)

■   ■   ■

My birth mother returned from school for the summer and found herself embarrassed. A note in the files describes the situation briefly: An "attractive, intelligent girl" was at university. She did not return in the autumn because her pregnancy, discovered over the summer, was threatening to show up herself and her family. Her family, being themselves well known in their community and subject to the rule of respectability, set her up, with complete disregard to irony, as a "mother's help" in a home far enough away for discretion.

After the child was born and the paperwork was done and the world resumed its mundane axis of lunatic regularity, she went abroad for the rest of the school year to further avoid discovery and discrimination; to safeguard herself, her future, and her family's reputation; her own little flight to Egypt.

By the time she returned, all danger would have passed, and no one would be any the wiser.

When we met, she told me quickly and carefully that she had no regrets.

The experts advised a gradual introduction: an exchange of letters leading, in time, to a phone call or two. We played along for a little while. I have photos of her family, hiking trails and looking at trains. I am sure I sent her pictures of our babies. But soon, very soon, there seemed little reason not simply to meet, to face one another.

By the time that we met, we were both the mothers of young children—her youngest was nine years old, and I had a three-year-old, a one-year-old, and my own youngest was making her presence known through hormonal communication: morning sickness, exhaustion, and tender breasts. I believe it helped that we had motherhood in common. As Mary and Elizabeth, meeting as relatives removed, family and familiar and yet almost as strangers, the shared gnosis of dark womb secrets lent a sisterhood to our meeting that erased embarrassment and undermined awkwardness with its own earthy, urgent reality.

We were still, for all intents and purposes, strangers to each other. I took the unnecessary precautions for meeting a stranger: arranged to meet in a public place (the railway station, lunch at a pub within walking distance). I left the children with a trusted friend. If all went well, I told her, we would come and pick up the children together after lunch. If not so well, I would pick them up alone.

All went well. "I want to say, 'You're here!'" my newly met mother said on the way to pick up the children after lunch, spreading her arms wide in an empty embrace.

Womanhood, in and of itself, can be exhausting. On top of that, opting in to motherhood seems an impetuous choice. Motherhood, whether biological or otherwise, accidental, assisted, or frustrated, requires a level of abandonment of one's body to another for a time (a longer time than anyone might reasonably anticipate) and may further require a certain disregard for whether that body will be returned to its owner in any recognizable shape. Any kind of parenting requires a certain suspension of daily calculations, of the overwhelming worries of the world. The kind of love that would sacrifice itself to keep a child together, that would argue with God over the terms of a loan, that would consider living through hell on earth a fair exchange for the privilege of parenting; such is the illogical call of motherhood.

God Herself appears as mother in the Bible, laboring her people to birth (see Isa. 42:14). As a mother, God is gentle as a hen who gathers her brood under her wings (see Luke 13:34) and as fierce and dangerous as a bear defending her cubs (see Hos. 13:8).

Mary, not exactly regretting her own impetuous assent to the angel's Annunciation, nevertheless ran with some haste to the hill country to greet her relative and shelter in her bosom, seeking some respite from the demands of everything that mattered less in time and space than that which she carried, wrought of mystery, with its own internal rhythm and logic; its own dark, slow pace; its own reason. When they met, it was the secrets of their wombs that bound them together in ecstasy and trembling. And Elizabeth greeted Mary,

"Blessed are you among women, and blessed is the fruit of your womb. And why has this happened to me, that the mother of my Lord comes to me? For as soon as I heard the sound of your greeting, the child in my womb leaped for joy. And blessed is she who believed that there would be a fulfillment of what was spoken to her by the Lord."

(Luke 1:42-45)

Questions for Reflection

- How do the biblical images of God as mother resonate with you? Do they expand, confirm, or redeem the idea of motherhood for you?

- Do you relate to God as a parent: mother, father, or other? If you have children, how do you relate God's parenting to your own?

- In order to become Incarnate, God, as Jesus, needed a mother. How does the intimacy of God's involvement with the human family affect your own intimacy with God?

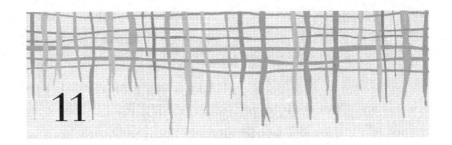

Choosing: Solomon

Solomon's reputation for wisdom is illustrated in the Bible's family court with a nightmare in vivid tones (see 1 Kings 3:16-28). A child has died. Another lives. Two women, both fresh from childbirth, with all the exhaustion and pain and wounded love that labor implies, claim the right to mother the surviving child. Solomon devises a cruel and twisted test to determine the truth. After he has rendered his judgment, the people stand "in awe of the king, because they perceived that the wisdom of God was in him, to execute justice" (1 Kings 3:28).

The word *execute* here may be a double-edged sword, and *awe* can be ambiguous. Choosing a family is no mean undertaking.

■   ■   ■

My parents fostered a small child long before they adopted one of their own. I have an old black and white photograph of him on the beach with my grandmother. He stayed with them for months. They considered him their son. They would have adopted him, but he was swept back into the world of social workers and muddy waters. A few months more, and our mother heard that he was in hot water again, something about a tea kettle, an arm, a scald, a cry. He was placed with another foster family.

I knew from before the time I could understand that I was adopted—I remember knowing, *I am adopted*, whilst simultaneously wondering, *What's "adopted"?* Our parents, learning from the errors of others, wisely made sure that my brother and I would never need to ask them, would never hear from a stranger or in the schoolyard that we were adopted. It was knowledge that we children grew into, that we had always known.

When we grew old enough to ask (as the family story is told) from the back seat of the car, out of thin air, what it meant, what had happened to us, we were told that we were born in love, and that it was out of love for us that our mothers had each chosen to find us a home, a family where we would have all that we needed. Like the mother in the Solomon story, willing to relinquish her child for the sake of his life, it was all for love, we were told, over and again. We were always loved.

Still, it seems there were details that our parents were less anxious to share. I was fascinated to find out only decades later that there was one more link in the archaeology of my origins: I had spent my first few weeks in a foster family. That was something we had never talked about at home.

I think that, for my mother, there was a grief involved in that loss of days, weeks, when I was else-where, someone else's child. Experience had taught her too that there was a whole world of danger out there, in those few missing weeks: tea kettles and tempers and attachments and bonding and who knew what. And it was a much less romantic story than that of their first baby, swept directly from the delivery ward and transported, stork-style, to our parents' waiting arms. Our parents described it as though they themselves were physically expectant: the excitement of knowing the baby was growing, not knowing when it would reveal itself to be a son or a daughter, ten fingers or toes. Knowing already that this was their child, sight unseen, they had fallen for the hope of him.

The court process was less romantic still. It took a few months, during which time his birth mother became less sure of her choice, wondered after all if she could face the shame cast on single motherhood in the 1960s, whether the hardships of that life would heal the hurt of losing her child.

Our mother entertained fantasies of running away with him, hiding in the hills, until it was too late, and he was irrevocably hers.

But the social workers were as practiced at persuading reluctant women that the deed was already done as they were at shuffling foster children. They could convince a woman that to reverse her decision would cause harm to one who had already bonded to another mother, a proper one with a husband, hearth, and home. They did not approve of independence, adultery, poverty. They made their choice clear and expected everyone to agree: Rather than break her child's heart, a real mother might be persuaded to harden her own, sign the papers, let him go.

■　■　■

Solomon was playing a dangerous game. If Solomon was wise enough, he would know that a mother's love can be as possessive as it can be permissive; as jealous as gentle; as passionate as pragmatic; as illogical as it can be lonely; as self-immolating as self-sacrificing. Mothers are not by definition paragons of virtue, models of the Madonna. Even Mary herself had moments of disinfatuation with her son, calling for the proverbial men in white coats to come and take him away if he would not stop his incessant preaching, his unintelligible proclamation of an unimaginable gospel. Mothers cannot always be relied upon to make the right choice for their child.

Read the paper. Watch the news. Be a child. Be a mother. Then revisit that scene in Solomon's court: Two women live together in a house of ill repute. In the night, both give birth. A single midwife divides her time between them, leaving each more or less alone to deliver her son, the wages of her work. An occupational hazard, the midwife calls it. Busy and brusque—this is not her hospital of choice—she swabs the mothers, swaddles the infants, doses everyone up, more or less, with sufficient pain relief to face the rest of the night, the panic of a new life stretched out before them, in dreamless peace. She leaves them to their own devices, promising to return by daylight, when it will be less dangerous to her own reputation to slip in and out of the shadows of the best-known hidden house in town.

But in the soft darkness of an emptying room, one mother accidentally smothers her child. One mother, too stupored to wake, dreams that her son has been stolen and replaced with a cold, lost boy. The morning light is a wakening nightmare. The midwife hears the scream from across town and shivers in her sleep. She saw them only by candlelight; she bathed them by touch more than sight; she will not have anything to do

131

with this tragedy. It is not of her making. She resolves to stay well away from the house today. These women made their beds, she reckons; finally, they must lie in them alone.

And what does the king see when these two women fight before him, hair strung out and spit flying from the corners of their mouths, hardly the sort he would usually entertain between his silk sheets? In my mind's eye, they look the same, from their long black hair, shiny with sweat from fighting, fever, and fear, to their maternal robes, loose and available, to their hungry hearts and full breasts. And each, you can rely on it, an exhausted and emotional, bereft and bleeding new mother, each wrung to the end of her wits to come this way before the king, before his court, before their betters, whom they knew well enough were no better than they ought to be, anyway.

Is the father of the living child among those gathered in the courtroom to see this spectacle? Is the father of the lost boy present? Are they the same man? Does he know, himself? A wise father knows his own child, but no one speaks up as Solomon declares his unutterable maternity test.

If Solomon is truly wise and not merely lucky or manipulative, then he does not dare to choose which woman is really a mother. I do not know, by this time, that even the women themselves are quite certain of their stories. If he is wise, Solomon can choose only the child.

Of course, he is the one who has put the poor mite in mortal danger. Let's hope the baby was too young to remember the flash of the sword; the guard's strong grip on his ankles; the panicked, animal screaming of one; the dull, numb grief of the other whom he might call mother.

Since the book does not name him, let's call him Forgetful, and pray that stands him in good stead.

■   ■   ■

My parents consistently, and before we were conscious of asking, told their children that we were loved; that the relinquishing of parental rights, claims, names could itself be an act of tender mercy and grace, an act of love. Like Solomon's subjects, we had no choice but to believe them.

Choosing is not an innocent concept when it comes to forming family. A choice implies that an alternative might have been equally viable. Choosing is not a neutral concept. In the early forms that accompany my adoption, there is evidence of a shift in emphasis. The local agency responsible for intake has changed its name. The *Moral Welfare Adoption Society* has scratched out its *Moral*s and replaced them with *Family*: the *Family*

Welfare Adoption Society recognizes that the choices we make for family reasons may be more ambiguous than clear cut.

At a certain point, friends become the family of choice for an uprooted generation. Changing economic and social dynamics divide families by the geography of jobs. It is an opportunity too for a generation to revolt (as each generation will) against the assumed authority of its elders. Perhaps even young Forgetful, the child chosen by default to be the son of the woman most likely to keep him alive, found his chance to choose a family for himself—one that better matched the vision in his heart of greatness, planted subliminally in the king's court the morning after his birth. Maybe he moved out of the unhappy house of his birth and chose to make his fortune or folly with his friends, brothers of circumstance. (He always felt as though he should have had a brother; as though there were a shadow, a forgotten twin, that haunted him. His mother did not like him to speak of it, and he used it, sometimes, against her.)

So much for fanciful thinking. But as far as the Bible goes, again, there is room at the family table, in the family tree, for ambiguity, and for choice. Ruth chose Naomi, hitching a ride on her skirts to the Promised Land and into the genealogy of Jesus (see the book of

Ruth; Matt. 1:5). Joseph chose to marry Mary instead of dismissing her quietly, as everyone in his family, from his mother to his maiden aunt, not to mention his bawdy uncle, must have advised him to do (see Matt. 1:18-21). For all that, when they came knocking at his door, Jesus made his own choice:

> "Who is my mother, and who are my brothers?"
> And pointing to his disciples, he said, "Here are
> my mother and my brothers!"
> (Matt. 12:48-49)

At the table on his last evening with his friends, before the unpleasantness in the garden and beyond, Jesus told them, "You did not choose me but I chose you" (John 15:16).

But because God's mercy endures forever, the next day, nailed to a cross, Jesus chose for his mother a new son, so that she would not be the one left alone with a dead child, uncomforted (see John 19:26-27).

Wisdom chooses love, executes it with frightening accuracy and clinical precision. No wonder we shrink from it, overcome with awe, blinded by its clarity, driven witless by its logic, chosen as her children.

■ ■ ■

Happy are those whom you choose and bring near
> to live in your courts.

We shall be satisfied with the goodness of your house,
> your holy temple.

(Ps. 65:4)

Questions for Reflection

- Whom have you chosen to be part of your family of faith?
- When did you know that God had chosen you to be part of God's family?

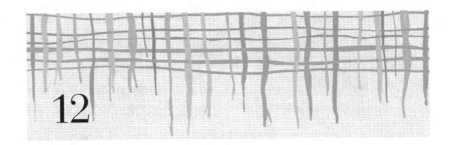

12

The Parable of Jephthah

A reading beside and between the lines: Jephthah grew up an outsider to his own family (see Judg. 11). His mother was, allegedly, a prostitute. His father either would not or could not, and at any rate did not, defend Jephthah against the outrage of his legitimate brothers, the sons of his father's wife. They purified the family, their parents' marriage with the fire of their most moral judgment, rescuing their mother's honor by driving the cuckoo out of the nest.

Jephthah became a cattle rustler and a sheep stealer and a bandit. He was good at it; so good, that when his brothers fell afoul of their neighbors and needed some muscle to come in and boost their military might, they thought of their rejected relative and the trouble he had caused throughout the region, and they wondered if he might cause some trouble on their behalf. They were after all, they reasoned, family.

Up to this point, the story is the one of the runt's redemption as hero; of the rejected stone becoming the cornerstone of the nation. It rehearses elements of the saga of Joseph and his brothers—the one who was sold away into slavery and ends up holding all the cards, and his brothers' fates, in his hand. Did Jephthah, like Joseph, dream of lording it over his brothers someday? The difference being that Jephthah has no doting father figure like Jacob waiting to embrace him. Jephthah gains the glory, but he is still out on his own.

The child Jephthah who was rejected spends a lifetime trying to earn his way back into his father's heart. He wants to earn his way back into his family's good graces, and he wants them to welcome him unconditionally. He wants to prove himself, yet he knows himself to be completely dependent upon his father's approval. He wants his brothers to owe him, and he wants to be equal to them. He grew up thinking that love was for barter. One cannot blame his mother; she never claimed that it was love she was selling. He mistook the bonds of family for stocks and bonds that could be bought and sold. He will never be done fighting for love while he is defending himself so rigorously against those who have withheld it from him for too long.

Jephthah's complicated relationship with his family is imprinted onto his petulant prayer to the Spirit of God at the head of his battle with the Ammonites: "Give me victory, give me glory, and I will give you anything. I will sacrifice the first thing I see when I get home" (see Judg. 11:29-33).

The irony is that Jephthah ends up sacrificing on the altar of his family's love and approval the only one who would do anything for him.

Jephthah's daughter adored her father. She was his greatest cheerleader. She knew of his insecurities and the complicated relationship he had with victory, joy, and his place in history because of his family's unkindness in his earlier years.

Or perhaps Jephthah's daughter was afraid of her father. She never knew which man would return from the war: the jovial conqueror made jaunty by victory or the sullen survivor, made brutal by battle.

But surely it must have been love that sent her dancing down the street to meet him like a woman, like a wife, channeling her foremothers, singing songs of celebration to praise him and to remind him to render unto God the glory due for his victory.[1] Such selfless love; she did not dispute her father's vow, nor even its fulfillment. She did not rail at him; she did not run away when he gave her the opening; she did not pass through the mountains and seek sanctuary with her uncles or with strangers. She had two months—more than the forty days elsewhere allotted in the Bible for big decisions and wilderness trials—to make up her mind to leave her father alone with his unkind promise, and instead, she came back to him. Her love ruined him: He killed her.

It is as though Jephthah—prodigal brother, importunate son, impetuous father—returned as one in a parable (see the parable of the prodigal, Luke 15:11-32). As though, finding his own father tremulous and his brothers still contemptuous, this returning prodigal took a torch from the fire under the fatted calf and burned the whole place down: any inheritance, any home, any family he might yet have hoped to enjoy.

I used to think that Jephthah would never pray again. But I wonder. Somehow, Jephthah continued living, judging Israel. (Never has that very word been a more finely sharpened, double-edged sword). Either he had inured himself so completely to life and grief that he continued like a zombie to lurch through its motions without a backward glance; or else her death, her murder at his hands, broke him so far open that he was ready at last to meet God on God's own terms, bereft and weeping for the warring spirits of humanity and the inhumanity of families to their own, wondering when the promised victory of love would be proclaimed.

Betrayed by his own unassuaged greed for love, Jephthah could have gone the way of Judas (see Matt. 27:3-10), or of David, who arose and washed his face when there was no hope left for his infant son, undone by his own adultery and murder (see 2 Sam. 12:15-23).

One could imagine alternative endings to the tragedy of Jephthah and his daughter. What if it had been Jephthah's father, waiting to congratulate his son, to embrace his homecoming hero, who ran first from the house to meet him on the road? He, family history implies, would surely not have allowed himself to become a burnt sacrifice. He would remind Jephthah that God always provides a ram, preferring that families fail to immolate one another in God's name.

What if the daughter had stayed in the hills forever, running with the mountain goats, fraternizing with shepherds, living out a fantasy of pastoral life, almost forgetting, over time, why she was afraid to descend into the valley on market day? A clean break.

Some family dysfunctions are too painful to relate or to resolve; too messy to come out clean.

Jephthah could go the way of Judas or of David; or, like the prodigal of Jephthah's parable, after he has burned it all down, he may find still the One who has always loved him sits in the ashes of their shared home, patient with anger and emotion, cold with love in the morning blue, waiting.

Questions for Reflection

- What stories from your family history are too difficult to tell? Would it help to process them with a trusted pastor or counselor?
- Where will you find God waiting for you in that process?

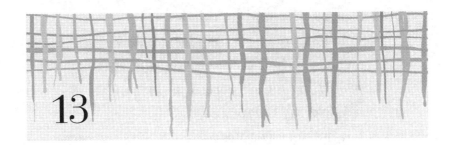

13

Birth and Baptism: "We Welcome You into the Household of God"

Quicken us, and we will call upon thy name.
—Psalm 80:18, KJV

■ ■ ■

You formed my inmost parts,
    linked liver to bile ducts,
        ankles to feet, unwebbed my toes,
    did something a little strange with my nose,
caused blood to flow, borrowed
    from my mother meat,
        installed a heart and made it beat.

Buried from view and unaided
    by our technological insight you saw
        what you had created from the earth
approaching a now perennial birth.
In your book, my blueprints,
    faded but serviceable, pressed
        like wildflowers into something,
a love letter, but to whom?
           —Psalm 139:13-16, wildly paraphrased

For the longest time in human history, the first received revelation of new life was the expectant mother's first experience of those surprising, fluttering sensations, like bubbles bursting against her belly, the first felt movements of an unborn child, conjuring up images of soft bones and unseeing fingers feeling their way into being. These first felt kicks and starts were known as "the quickening." While a woman may have known for some little while that something was up, and growing, it was considered by scholars and sages that the quickening indicated God's intervention, secretly inserting a soul into the fetus and bringing it to life.

We seldom hear the language any more of "the quick and the dead," but as slow as I was to understand it as a child, it became evocative of the mysteries of life implanted in us; something scurrying and unsearchable. It speaks of the divine wisdom that inspires a quick and inquiring mind, one that is restless in its search for meaning, for connection, for love. It speaks to the vulnerability of one who may be cut to the quick by hurt administered, casual or cruel unkindness, love withheld. It is language that speaks of hope and fear to an expectant parent.

The Psalms seek the mystery of that quickening, that ensoulment that is God's responsibility alone; the continuing creation of clay creatures animated by the breath of the Holy Spirit, as though the psalmist were uncertain of any identity beyond that bequeathed by the image of God, as though seeking reassurance that we are real, after all, modeled after a real God.

At school, someone told me that everything in a person is a product of ingredients provided first by genetics, then shaped and "cooked" by environment and upbringing. We are nothing more, he told me, than the sum of the parts bequeathed to us by our parents. He may be right; little enough in this life seems beyond the influence of accidents. For instance, my name has changed. One leg is longer than the other, and a little turned outward; the result, I am certain, of falling down the stairs as a greenstick-boned infant and then hanging up in traction in a hospital crib. My mother described unwinding me, like a twisted sheet, each time she came to visit. Even my face is not the one I was born with. When I took our eldest daughter to the orthodontist for braces, he explained that unlike when I was young, they don't remove teeth any more from crowded jawlines. "We don't want to change her lovely, strong bone structure," he told me. I went home and put my hands to my head before the mirror, no longer sure of it. Even the voices in that altered head can be traced back to scratchy, jumpy, repetitious recordings of other people's memories, for the most part.

All of this, the simple sum of nature and nurture, genes, injury, and environment, a simple equation calculated to output an accidental woman. But there is something in me that is not quite willing to submit to a randomly engineered existence. With the psalmist I might argue, with all due respect to those magicians, that God is more than a mechanic, hooking up organs and cleaning out fuel pipes, fixing generators, tuning up timings, calibrating competing pressures, and switching on souls.

"And so it is written, The first man Adam was made a living soul; the last Adam was made a quickening spirit" (1 Cor. 15:45, KJV). Is it too much to consider that we are such stardust creatures, blown about on the atmosphere, tossed salads of DNA and defining experience; and that still, even so, God causes in each one of us a quickening, a new dimension to life, beyond accident?

We know that the whole creation has been groaning in labor pains until now; and not only the creation, but we ourselves, who have the first fruits of the Spirit, groan inwardly while we wait for adoption, the redemption of our bodies.

(Rom. 8:22-23)

Is it too much to believe that it is God's quickening spirit that leaps within us when we hear the greeting of the mother of God and of the fruit of her womb, Jesus; God's quickening Spirit, which was from the beginning brooding over the waters of Creation, telling the tale of the thread and threat of water as life; the briny amniotic fluid of our birth; the borrowed holy water of our baptism?

∷ ∷ ∷

In the beginning, when everything that was yet to come was formless and void, something unseen, unimagined, uncreated brooded over the waters of the deep, like a diaphragm moving up and down, creating waves on the surface of a womb, but untethered, freely hovering in mid-void, like a breathless pterodactyl or an albatross, or a dove not yet scaled down to fit within a creation not yet scaled up. It did not ride the currents of the wind, for as yet there was none, except for that which was created by the movement of its own wings, changing the changelessness of eternity, creating out of a vacuum atmosphere, air; something to vibrate, the prehistory of music, of birdsong, so that God could speak the next line aloud: *Let there be light* (see Gen. 1:1-3).

Millennia later, perhaps it experienced some déjà vu, tumbling through the storm, a wild ride; the darkness as encompassing as eternity, the waters as wild and chaotic as though they had never been tamed and tailored into seas. But this time, there was sound, a noise like never before, thunder and gales, the orchestral extravagance of atmosphere. And there was an ark.

If indeed the Winged One visited, Noah never seemed to notice that he ended up with three doves. The one, so eager to give evidence of life, bears witness to the burgeoning of a new creation, an olive twig; this one, having done its duty, breathing hope back into Noah's lead lungs, pneumoniac after months of inhaling rain; now this one escaped back to whence it had come, and no one who had counted the birds twice passed comment on the interloper, the "third wing" (see Gen. 8:1-12).

Some time passed, as will every creature. The hovering winged thing rehearsed its opening song one night, accompanied by angels. Some called it the music of the spheres; others thought it some new song, strange and beautiful, come to birth.

Still, it was drawn to the water, falling with ecstasy upon the man dripping with baptism, scattering blessings as a dog shakes water from its bath. As though jealous over its watery domain, the dove bit and pecked him until he retreated to the dry desert wilderness (see Mark 1:9-12).

This time, the dove stayed on for a while; but being earthbound was dispiriting. It found itself caged, pressed into service as sacrifice. The blessing man came across it by chance one day, as he was sweeping through the Temple, and set it free once more (see John 2:13-16).

Burned out on air and water, after a brief respite, it thought it might have a go with fire (see Acts 1:4-5; 2:1-4).

■　　■　　■

It was Mothering Sunday, kept on the fourth Sunday of Lent in the Church of England. We were packing up the house to move to Singapore. I included the two smocked dresses, hand-me-downs from my half-sisters, dug out of her attic by my birth mother.

In the midst of lists of paperwork and making arrangements for the cat, there was another matter that needed attending to before I was ready to leave the country for the unknown. We had a baby to baptize, and by Easter we would be gone; so, we chose Mothering Sunday to celebrate, and we invited all the family.

We should have done it at the morning service we attended every week, but I had invited both of my mothers, and my birth mother's mother. My mother-in-law would be there and the baby's other godmother. I had not yet met my maternal grandparents; none of the extended family members had met one another.

I was more than a little overwhelmed.

I asked our priest, a good friend, if we could have a quieter service in the afternoon. There would be breathing room; space for us to circle one another, find our way toward one another slowly, all of these different shades of mothers and daughters, brothers and sisters, and strangers. It isn't the way we like to do a parish baptism, but this time, feeling our way into becoming family, it seemed like a good idea.

That Sunday, the baby had a cold. She was miserable and fretful, although she could have been picking up the jitters from me. I met so many family members for the first time that afternoon. There was a mess of hugging, kissing, and crying going on. My biological grandfather asked, not unreasonably, "Why are we hugging all these strangers?" He seemed bemused by the familiarity of family that had never before met. My parents surprised me by presenting my birth mother with a photograph album: copies of the milestone moments from the day they adopted me through the day of my wedding, the official and traditional graduation from their home to one of my own.

An Orthodox priest once told me that in his tradition, the relationships formed through baptism were equivalent to those by birth or adoption. My child, for example, could not marry my godchild any more than she could marry her own sister.

I had not yet heard this version of the family dynamic when I invited my birth mother to become godmother to her grandchild, but on an instinctive level, it made sense; the family of the church offered an alternative way of being family to one another, unencumbered by history and its wounds, or its expectations, or its need for awkward explanations.

Her grandmother became her godmother, her great-grandfather her great-godfather; her elementary-school-aged aunt became her godsister.

The fact that my mothers' names were Ann and Anne led to a mild comedy of errors among the less-related guests at the reception in the church hall, trying to work out which mother was which. In even more of a coincidence, each woman had one brother, both named John. The Uncle John I had grown up knowing was not there. In fact, I did not see him again before he died of heart failure on Christmas Day of the following year. The uncle John whom I had never yet met was the family historian. He had been a teenager when I was born, and his parents had protected him from the dangerous knowledge of his sister's dilemma so that it wouldn't affect his grades at school. They had always assumed that she would one day tell him; she thought they had. Despite the rude surprise I presented to his careful histories, he was with us for the baptism too. He came bearing a sweet gift for the baby: honey in the comb, harvested from his own bees. We ate it by the spoonful, the children and I, cleaning out the jar in the week and a half we had left before moving to the far side of the world.

We hold a tradition that John the Baptizer, who ate wild honey (which, incidentally, grows on trees, not bees), was some kind of a cousin to Jesus through their mothers, but we don't really know to what degree or how many times removed. We see them together only in their mothers' wombs and once more when they gather at the river for baptism with the water rolling hot and sluggish past them as they contemplate the divine mystery that has led them here.

There is a thread, quite apart from the genealogies and genetic markers that run in endless lists through the history of our spiritual ancestors. There is a thread that links drops of water in a flood; there is a Spirit, brooding over the deep waters, which are without form, and void, before the creation of the world.

It is related to the dove that brings its olive branch to Noah, a sign of God's peace. In some form, it taps Hagar on the shoulder, showing water in the well for her son, Ishmael; the watercourses of the Negev. It holds Jacob to his promise of a new life, a new name, in the Jabbok River; draws Moses from the water, helps him strike water from the rock. It parts seas and rivers for the prophets, making their pathways straight, leading them on solid ground. There is a river that flows from the throne of God, and over its currents, enjoying the lift and play of the air, I imagine the Spirit swooping, and diving, resting and blessing, now as then, the sacrifice of baptism.

My friend, our priest, used to joke that while the old prayer book tells the parents to hand the baby over to him, it never does instruct the priest to give her back. And there was a feeling almost of sacrifice in this ritual of offering up this baby for the sake of the family, for the sake of bringing us together; of giving her over to God, to her godparents—in that moment of handing her over to receive the sacrament of baptism.

And the congregation now responds, "We receive you into the household of God."[1]

■   ■   ■

Our youngest child cried before she was fully born. As soon as her face was free and clear, she pulled in her breath and wailed the rest of her little form out from the birth canal. It was, as you may imagine, the strangest sensation to hear the new and independent voice of my child before she had left my body.

It is as though we are born crying out already for God. With our first breath, before we have even left the womb, we know our source of being. We know whose child we are. Deeper than memory, thicker than blood, stronger even than love, as it is limited by human imagination. The Spirit of our adoption is the one that cries with the newborn child; that weeps with the bereaved parent; that rejoices in tears with the restored family; that baptizes us before we know ourselves with the quickening Spirit of God, so that our souls cry out, "Abba."

This child was born with the womb waters backed up behind her, so that she was washed clean by the wave that followed her through the birth canal, into the world. That Mother's Day, she was washed again in the waters of baptism, born into a new family. It is by an act of faith that we offer our children up, we who are parents, godparents, foster families, formal and informal guardians by faith. We stand around the font or the baptistry with Abraham and Sarah; Hagar and Hannah; David, Bathsheba, and the ghost of Uriah; with Mary, Joseph, and Jesus, who loved all the little children. He had none to call his own but many to bear his name. It is by faith that we offer them up and by an act of grace that they are returned to us, the same, but changed, watermarked; marked forever as belonging to and with a family beyond our reckoning.

Not long after the baby's baptism, we moved overseas, to the other side of the world. The Sunday before we left, the priest used us as an illustration in his sermon. Sending us to stand in the furthest corner of the room, he promised that we would still be one with the family of Christ; that some bonds remain unbroken by distance or change, by a new home, accent, or language. That we would be, forever, one family under God.

Questions for Reflection

- When you consider the many mansions or dwelling places that are prepared for us in God's household, what images are conjured up in your faithful imagination?
- Who is living there? Who is missing?
- Where is God?
- How have your answers changed from when you began reading this book?

ACKNOWLEDGMENTS

There are too many people to thank by name for their part in the creation of this book to do them all justice. From Doug, Dilwyn, Peter, Ian, Pam, and the rest of All Saints, a great cloud of witnesses has buoyed my faith. I am grateful to my bishops, especially The Rt. Rev. Mark Hollingsworth Jr., and to other colleagues, particularly Evan, Ken, and Jon; to the Rev. Steve Secaur, who helped provide me with sabbatical time to write; and to the congregation of Epiphany, Euclid, whom I serve as Rector, who are a constant source of support and encouragement. Joy, who appears in chapter 6, died on Christmas Day. She continues to be for me an example of faith; love; and, yes, great joy.

The hospitality of the Collegeville Institute, the skill of its instructors, and the companionship of its community have been a blessing. Communities of writers, online and in person, such as Phil Fox Rose, many RevGalBlogPals, and others have been a Godsend, answering questions and offering wisdom.

Acknowledgments

Joanna Bradley Kennedy, Joseph Crowe, J. Dana Trent, and Christina Kukuk, my writing partner, know how many words I owe them.

I have been humbled by the love and forbearance of my family. I wish Mum could have read this book; I am profoundly grateful to Dad and to Anne for so many of the stories I have to tell.

To my husband, Gareth, and our offspring, Freya, Edward, and Megan: Thank you. I love you. You know the rest of the story.

NOTES

Introduction: Many Mansions

1. Saint Augustine, *Confessions*, Book I.

Chapter 1—All in the Family: Abraham, Isaac, and Lot

1. See Karen Armstrong, *In the Beginning: A New Interpretation of Genesis* (New York: Alfred A. Knopf, 1996), 71.

Chapter 3—Complications: Rachel Unconsoled

1. See *The New Oxford Annotated Bible*, 3rd ed., Michael D. Coogan, ed., Marc Z. Brettler, Carol A. Newsom, Pheme Perkins, assoc. eds. (Oxford, England, UK: Oxford University Press, 2001), Numbers 5:11-31, 193 Hebrew Bible, notes on the text.

Chapter 5—Genealogies

1. *The New Interpreter's Bible Commentary, Volume VIII* (Nashville, TN: Abingdon Press, 1994), 125–26.

Chapter 7—Family Politics: Moses

1. Wilda C. Gafney, *Womanist Midrash: A Reintroduction to the Women of the Torah and the Throne* (Louisville, KY: Westminster John Knox Press, 2017), 99–100.
2. Gafney, *Womanist Midrash,* 99–100.
3. Gafney, *Womanist Midrash,* 99–100.
4. Gafney, *Womanist Midrash*, 93.
5. "God loves you. No exceptions.®" is a tagline and registered trademark of the Episcopal Diocese of Ohio.

Chapter 8—Family and Other Animals

1. James Strong, *Strong's Exhaustive Concordance* (Nashville, TN: Abingdon Press, 1890, thirty-second printing, 1974), 175.

Chapter 12—The Parable of Jephthah

1. Tikva Frymer-Kensky, *Reading the Women of the Bible: A New Interpretation of Their Stories* (New York: Schocken Books, 2002), 108.

Chapter 13—Birth and Baptism: "We Welcome You into the Household of God"

1. The Book of Common Prayer, 309.